More Than You Ever IMAGINED

❧❀❧

THE ASTONISHING JOURNEY TO SEXUAL ENLIGHTENMENT

❧❀❧

More Than You Ever IMAGINED

THE ASTONISHING JOURNEY TO SEXUAL ENLIGHTENMENT

KRISTIN LISH

Core Synergies

More Than You Ever Imagined
The Astonishing Journey to Sexual Enlightenment
By Kristin Lish
Copyright © 2008 by Kristin Lish

Core Synergies
P.O. Box 540341
North Salt Lake, Utah 84054

Orders and Information at www.MoreThanYouEverImagined.com

Copy Editor: Shelly Jensen
Copy Editor: Dana Stohlton
Typesetting: Megan Duncan
Cover Design: Tina Falk

Library of Congress Cataloging-in Publication Data

Lish, Kristin
More than you ever imagined: the astonishing journey to sexual enlightenment/
ISBN: 978-0-6152-0665-3

Author's Note
Because everyone's beliefs and experiences are unique, the suggestions and ideas contained herein should not be considered a substitute for consultation with a trained therapist or enlightened spiritual counselor.

*To Mom and Dad
and cousin Candy*

꩜

CONTENTS

Acknowledgements

I humbly offer my love and appreciation to the following people who played an important role in the creation of this book. It has been a great collaborative effort of many enthusiastic and committed supporters, reviewers, editors, and designers—all who helped light the path.

Farrel and Ruth Lish	Richard and Sherrie Contreras	Betty Budack
Mikel Glade	Tyler and Marni Henderson	Mark Neihart
Dr. Craig Buhler	Glenn and Colleen Buhler	Dan Murdock
Carol Hansen	Cynthia Black	John Miller
Sharon Moran	Ja-lene Clark	Dr. Gene Nelson
Angela Soper	Michele Clarkson	Dr. Juliana Dahl
Nedra Robbins	Tina Falk	Anne Sproat
Megan Duncan	Gary Scott	Brent Undhjem
Sylvia Nibley	Dana Stohlton	Alice Tanita
Bill and Candy Fowler	Tim Hansen	

To my beloved parents—without you this book could never have been written. Thank you for deeply loving me. I miss you so much.

To my beautiful daughters, Mikel and Marni—there is so much I wanted to give to you but couldn't when I was raising you alone. However, our lives together have birthed the heart of this inspired book! May it bring you peace and joy. I love you so much.

To my sister, Sherrie—how could I get along in life without your constant support and encouragement? Thank you for protecting me all my life.

To my lifelong friend, Colleen—thank you for faithfully believing in me and steadfastly supporting the completion of this book.

To my Heavenly Family—I offer my eternal gratitude for your guidance, love, revelation, and inspiration, and for teaching me how to write and share this book with the world.

❧❦❧

BEFORE YOU BEGIN
YOUR JOURNEY

I gratefully and excitedly dedicate this book to all who are embarking on the extraordinary and essential journey of sexual enlightenment. There are no prerequisites and no restrictions. Age, gender, health, sexual orientation, religious or spiritual beliefs, nationality, and all other classifications—whether we come by them naturally or carefully choose them for ourselves—do not have any bearing on this journey. All are equal and worthy members of our pilgrimage.

As brave pioneers, our success can and will positively change the world forever. Human beings have been preparing for this evolution in consciousness for thousands of years. Based on the universal truths of energy and love, this worldwide evolution is more than a quest; it is our spiritual right and responsibility. Through self-discovery—understanding who we are, why we are here, and where we are going—we can embrace our inherent right and responsibility and sow the seeds of sexual enlightenment.

Now is the time to embrace a new sexual paradigm, to empower not just our physical bodies, but also our energy bodies. While astounding scientific advances are providing existential evidence of energy, technological advances, especially the Internet, are proliferating increasingly destructive sexual practices, making sexual enlightenment imperative. Achieving this dramatic shift in consciousness necessitates that we accept and honor the divine source, nature, and many natural gifts of sexual energy.

Healthy sexuality offers us pleasure, love, and deepened intimacy, but sexual enlightenment takes us to another level of love and ecstasy, offering more than we ever imagined. Envision what would happen to the human race if each person's profoundly unique gifts to the world were discovered and consciously developed and nurtured without fear and limitation. What if we used our expanded minds and hearts to identify the highest good for human beings, for all Earth's beings? How would the world's governmental and business structures change? What new goals for world health and peace could we achieve with new scientific and technological advancements? Geniuses of the heart and mind would be common so how might they use art, music, literature, film, and other forms of communication to inspire and free the world of shame and destruction? And perhaps the most exciting question of all—how would all future generations of human beings live because their ancestors came out of the dark ages of sexuality? Consciously transmuting and responsibly guiding the divine energy within—sexual enlightenment—is the next phase of human evolution, and you can help create it.

There are many reasons why people choose to explore and learn the new paradigm of sexuality offered in this book. Parents, grandparents, and caretakers of small children and teenagers may want to protect, educate, and inspire their young charges with the truth about sexuality. Beloved partners may feel sexually frustrated and bored, or maybe they feel sexually healthy and satisfied, but desire to learn how to be better lovers. Healthcare professionals may need to gain insights that enable them to successfully help patients who struggle with the physical issues of sexuality. Sex therapists may wish to gain a broader picture of sexuality so they can offer more effective guidance to their clients.

Many women and men may want to gain a better understanding of the opposite sex so they can deepen and strengthen their relationships, while others, especially women, may find it difficult to open up to sexual expression because of repression. Likewise, victims of sexual violence, and even the perpetrators of such heinous tragedies, may desperately need to reclaim their sexual health. Those who struggle with addictions to sexually obsessive behaviors such as prostitution and pornography, which are especially problematic for men, may be urgently searching for a way out of the darkness so they can save their relationships and lead productive lives.

Those in the winters of their lives may want spiritual tools to help them embrace peace with their past and present as they prepare for passing. Some people may be passionately looking for ways to give back to humanity, to manifest goodness and prosperity in their lives. Perhaps those who are clergy members feel their knowledge and counseling about sexuality is inadequate and want to be enlightened. Conversely, those who received inadequate spiritual and religious counseling may feel deep sexual shame that greatly needs to be released. Others may feel deep shame about their sexual orientation. Some people may be physically unable to express themselves sexually due to injuries and disease, but yearn to understand and experience the power of healthy sexual energy. On the other hand, those who choose to be celibate may desire to connect with their inner masculine and feminine energies and the divine.

Perhaps those who are women long to know and express what it really means to be a woman, or those who are men strive to feel and exhibit confidence, focus, and strength in the world. Some individuals may be preparing for marriage and sexual intimacy and want to know how they can successfully make these life-changing transitions. On the other hand, some may be ending a marriage or relationship and need to understand what went wrong and how they can prepare to successfully choose a new life and partner. Teenagers may want to better understand gender and sexual energy.

In this day and age, women often lose touch with their feminine essences. Are you such a woman? Men are often concerned about erectile dysfunction and premature ejaculation. Are you such a man? Are you looking for alternatives to prescription drugs that cause side effects that inhibit your sexual health? Are you a woman who is non-orgasmic? Are you a government leader who wants to more deeply live from a foundation of integrity and honorable purpose? Are you a new mother who wants to regain a sense of ownership of your body and open again to sexual expression? Do you feel an intense desire to change the world for the better? Are you searching for personal truth, spiritual guidance, and divine revelation? Do you want to learn to change your sexual energy and commune with the divine? Do you want to be the best lover possible? Have you heard about the spiritual nature of sexuality and want to learn all you can?

Regardless of why you want to become sexually enlightened, the most important thing to remember is that your quest is possible! The information contained in this book offers a common ground of understanding for humankind, making it applicable to all who seek enlightenment. The ideas are seemingly radical and profoundly new, yet instinctively familiar and sacred. Use these carefully presented theories, techniques, and practices as your compass so you can successfully navigate your personal and unique sexual journey. To further help you, eight enlightened expressions of sexual energy are presented with compelling detail. Personal qualities for facilitating a successful and safe passage are suggested and their use encouraged throughout the book.

Though the author offers a deeply inspired message of healing, hope, and enlightenment, she is simply a dedicated messenger.

ABOUT THE AUTHOR

I am an author, sex educator, and spiritual counselor in sexuality, a workshop facilitator, a speaker, and a musician. I have lived and worked in many places around the world, offering workshops and private sessions to thousands of people to help them transform their lives and embrace the depth and fullness of life's possibilities. I serve as an outlet for them to talk about sexuality in a safe and insightful manner, to understand and learn to create shame-free, spiritual-based sexuality. They are also drawn to my book and other resources because they hear or read the words "spiritual energy" in relation to sexual energy and are fascinated. Instinctively, they recognize the core of their sexuality is, in truth, spiritual. They want to learn more. They want to awaken. Their interest and inspiration give them courage to begin to open up, create, heal, and transform.

I also work with leaders and members of religious organizations, as well as leaders and employees of businesses and corporations, teaching them about the flow of energies within and between people. What's more, I help them learn how to transmute sexual energy in order to ignite the brilliance and creative process of the mind and to set and obtain worthy, inspiring goals for themselves and the world.

People often ask me why I do this kind of work and what led me to it. They want to know what in my personality prompted me to do work that takes me to the outer fringes of what is acceptable to society. Sometimes they warn me that other people might misunderstand what I do and try to discredit or even hurt me. Overall, they wonder why I work with such abandon and believe in it so much.

I explain to them that I believe every person in the world has a special gift to offer and that knowing and accepting the responsibility for sharing that gift is perhaps one of life's deepest sources of peace and contentment. It takes great courage, hard work, inspiration, and, oftentimes, pain and despair or a lifetime before the answer is revealed—before a person understands with certainty why his or her gift is unique.

Hence, I work in the field of sexuality because it is my special gift to offer to the world. I wouldn't be fulfilled if I denied it, though I spent decades finding that clarity. My work in sexuality is my life's purpose. I offer this vital, moving work because I believe it is my spiritual calling.

For most of my adult life, I have listened to the inner voice of a vague, distant drum—an indescribable, powerful yearning that would eventually lead me to explore various cultures around the world, diverse spiritual and religious traditions, and many splendid, sacred places on Earth. Throughout my explorations, I was introduced to wonderful books, marvelous and tender animals, and amazing human beings. I was also blessed and honored with two beautiful daughters. I am profoundly thankful for my many blessings, and I want to give back all that I can. I love life.

While I have experienced wonderful blessings, I have also experienced grave personal illness and tragedy, destructive sexual trauma, and devastating wounds to my feminine essence. Therefore, I offer my gifts in the field of sexuality to others because I do not want them to suffer the way I suffered. For example, I do not want people to see their marriages destroyed because they don't know how to talk about sexual and intimate issues. I don't want people to experience the life destroying effects of deep, toxic shame and injuries related to sexual abuse. I don't want people to suffer because they don't clearly understand and gracefully love or honor gender differences.

The seeds for my life's work and the creation of this book were planted when I was a little girl. The things I loved and trusted the most provided me with the tools I needed to expose the things I despised and feared the most—not only as a five year old, but also throughout my life. As a child, I loved the warm desert sand; the brilliant sun; the old sap-oozing trees; the noisy, happy birds; and the soft, gentle lizards. They were my best friends. Beauty was my teacher and inspiration. I joyfully embraced music, dance, animals, rivers, and mountains. I felt very safe with my family and relatives. I deeply loved Jesus and wanted him to be my best friend, and I painfully sobbed with the thought of him being hurt. I also believed in the angels that I could feel and hear around me.

However, I feared our neighbor who lived a few houses away. I was repulsed by the sight and smell of him. I was afraid that if I didn't behave well, he would hurt my parents. I thought he was too big, and I didn't trust his crooked smile. I despised the way he touched his wife and daughters. I feared walking past the little dark room beside his garage, but could never quite remember why. In time, though, the answer would call to me. And so my sexual wounds began when I was five years old, but decades would pass before I consciously began to remember them. Gratefully, fate led me into remembrance through a safe and timely opening.

I was walking on a Persian Gulf beach in Saudi Arabia when a friendly, beautiful Western woman came up and started talking to me. We visited, laughed, and shared as we walked. There was an instant comfort that amazed us. We learned that both of us had arrived from the United States with our husbands only two weeks prior. We both loved music, dance, mountains, and horses. Each of us had children of our own, as well as a background in teaching. At the end of the visit, we discovered an even more profound similarity—we were born the same year, month, day, and minute. Essentially, our mothers were pushing us out of the birth canal at the same time. Furthermore, it would only take us days before we would remember and begin to share our lonely and dark secrets of experiencing sexual trauma.

As women sensitive to energy in the physical body, our following three years in Saudi Arabia were spent helping each other release the emotional, spiritual, mental, physical, and energetic trauma of sexual wounding. We were graced. Our gods helped us save each other. Our lives would never be the same, though the miraculous bond of twin-sisterhood would never change. In the future, we would further our academic interests at the same time, on the same subject, and at the same graduate school—both of us are currently teaching in the field of sexuality.

Following this intense period of healing in Saudi Arabia, I entered graduate school and completed a master's degree in psychology. I began to articulate the need to free myself from Western culture's distorted, shallow, and usually negative beliefs and values related to sexuality. For many years, I had asked and examined the question: What is the contemporary experience of exploring and honoring a sacred relationship with my body and the Earth, and, in the deepest sense, what does it mean to be a woman? I had explored the issues, not because I was uncomfortable with my femininity, but because I sensed that I could find a fuller and deeper meaning and that it would dramatically change my life. As a child and teenager, I had not been introduced to divine models for femininity so I instinctively felt unsettled in my adult life. I sensed something profoundly meaningful was absent; I wasn't whole. I craved the exploration of new meanings. I was eager and wildly devoted to transforming my life.

> *Beginning with the writing of my first paper in graduate school, something most unexpected occurred. I began to feel, hear, and relate to the presence of a ghostlike inner energy. Each time it "spoke" to me, it did so with an increasingly demanding and burning intensity. Finally, with the silent power of its primordial scream, it not only took possession of my computer, my fingers, and my mind, but also my heart, my mouth, and my tears. It called forth the cries and moans of muted self, rising in me like a great white tidal wave of vagueness, searching for land, for embodiment—demanding recognition, demanding articulation, demanding presence. The she-ghost called to me from deep between my eyes, in the center of my brain. I followed her into my heart, through an open door in my back, and out into the Fields of Mystery. She consumed me as she entered through my gut, ran down both legs, and plummeted into and around Earth, anchoring me like a womb weed gone wild. I offered no resistance.*
>
> *I long for meaningful words. I long for meaningful life.*
>
> —An Excerpt from the Author's Journal

The longing was acknowledged and graced. Consequently, part of my academic research involved spending extended periods of time alone in the desert in order to experience and explore a relationship with Earth. My worldview is not necessarily compatible with the worldview of those who consider the traditionally accepted scientific method of research as the only valid form of inquiry. However, anthropological evidence shows that countless women and men through prehistory and history have experienced a deep sense of communication with nature and with specific non-humans. Therefore, I did not question the existence of spiritual communication between humans and other beings, but rather I wanted to know how to study and deepen those kinds of relationships. And so, the academic research began.

I simply walked into the desert wilderness, expressing my intention to seek communion with Earth's nature while quietly using my outer and inner eyes and ears. When I felt a special calling, whether it was from a tree, rock, boulder, bird, wind, or shadow, I stopped walking and sincerely, silently prayed for guidance and talked to Earth.

As I more consciously became a receptive vessel and intently listened, my perceptions changed and my awareness expanded. My deep, full breathing was the key to expanding that consciousness because it dissolved normal boundaries. Entering into a creative void or relationship with the unknown requires a total trust in oneself and the divine nature of the universe; simultaneously, it requires a complete letting go of any need to control the outcome, yet faith that one will be guided and protected during the process. As a musician and composer, and as a person profoundly sensitive to life energy, this creative process was completely familiar to me. For decades, I had totally trusted the process.

Whether I was expressing thankfulness, feeling oneness with other species, or communing with the Earth, the natural structure of my sentences was simple—though I did not deliberately simplify them. When my experiences were so profound they could not be contained and expressed in the English language, I automatically and instinctively started to cry, speak, sing, or chant in another form of communication to enable communion to take place. I documented all of these experiences with a handheld tape recorder and later transcribed every word and sound.

I have chosen to share my academic process of inquiry with you for several reasons. First, I want the unusual communications—the mystical and transformational experiences—to be acknowledged and claimed in words because they set the foundation for future exploration and teachings of healthy, spiritual, and erotic sexual expression. Second, I believe an intimate relationship with Earth is essential for anyone who wants to explore healthy sexuality. Third, my experiences are an example of a process I firmly believe is critical. Humans cannot come out of the dark ages of sexuality if they do not open their minds and hearts and willingly take the personal journey into exploration and transformation. Every person has a distinct path that must be honored. The transformation may not be easy; it takes determination, courage, and perhaps a lifetime of exploration and perseverance. Each person's individual creative process must be enlivened, nurtured, and protected, and will most likely involve redefining his or her relationship with religion and spirituality.

My growth and healing certainly involved redefining my relationship with religion and spirituality. Because of unacknowledged shame, I felt confused about the religion of my birth—my Christian roots. As a result, I spent most of my adult life traveling to many places in the world trying to resolve an inner turmoil I couldn't even name. Hence, I was drawn to and studied the world's major religions as well as other spiritual philosophies such as Earth-based spirituality, animism, shamanism, paganism, and Wicca. At the same time, I was miraculously drawn to a new understanding and expression of sexuality.

At the core of the vast and diverse spiritual traditions I studied, I discovered a hidden message that spirituality is in essence erotic and sexuality is in essence spiritual. These universal truths taught me that I could not realize the full potential of my sexual love and ecstasy without fully understanding the spiritual depths of my erotic nature. Likewise, I could not realize the full potential of my spirituality without relating it to my sexuality.

In time, and with persistence and courage, I was able to heal and transform my sexual and spiritual life. I learned how to positively, lovingly, joyfully, and deeply express my sexual and spiritual energies. Through many years of practicing the spiritual tool of sexual celibacy, I learned to open up and merge my sexual energy with divine love and power. Once I understood the source and nature of sexual energy, I was able to receive its many natural gifts. Inspired by spiritual guidance, I learned how to transmute sexual energy in order to heal my body and receive personal inspiration and revelation.

Equally as important, I also renewed my relationship with the religious doctrines and traditions of my Christian roots because I acknowledged and healed deep shame. As the years passed, I found that no matter where my powerful need for freedom led me in the world, my wings could always carry me home to my heart, the beloved religion of my birth—my eternal roots. Feeling that truth created a tender appreciation and peace I had never known.

Additionally, and to my amazement, I found I was part of a small group of people around the world that was making the same inner journey into an awakened spiritual relationship with sexuality. I sought participation. I found meaningful contribution. Gratefully, I began helping others do the same thing.

Presently, I share what I have learned during my lifelong journey with as many people as possible, regardless of their spiritual and religious beliefs. They discover what I discovered: the astonishing journey to sexual enlightenment is more than we ever imagined!

SPIRITUALITY AND RELIGION

The relationship of sexual energy and spiritual energy is a constant theme in this book. Consequently, you will be exploring two of the most personal ideas and feelings you could ever share with another person. Furthermore, your sexual enlightenment is explicitly tied to your ability to acknowledge and relate to a power wiser and stronger than yourself. Because a relationship with spirituality and religion is every human being's right and responsibility to define, this book offers no definitions for a higher power. What's more, this book honors all religious and spiritual beliefs, traditions, and practices, but none are elevated or explored. By necessity and for convenience and simplicity, the words "Divine Masculine," "Divine Feminine," and "God" are used to encompass the diversity and complexity of all religious and spiritual beliefs. Therefore, personalizing the meanings of the words is as necessary for you as personalizing the expressions of your sexual energy.

SHAME AND GUILT

In every journey to unexplored regions of inner and outer worlds, the possibility of encountering danger is ever present. Be aware—confusing and troubling thoughts and feelings may be lurking in the shadows of your heart or someplace else! Deep feelings of shame and guilt can be very stressful and even treacherous. Perilous, unacknowledged and unreleased shame could delay or end your journey out of darkness toward the light of joyous understanding. Furthermore, unresolved issues with religious and spiritual structures and philosophies are the number one reason people do not obtain sexual fulfillment. Some people have deep sexual wounding they are not aware of or don't understand. Likewise, some people do not experience the effects of destructive shame. Nonetheless, it is highly recommended that you learn and apply the powerful, spiritual tool for identifying and releasing shame as outlined in Chapter 4—Shame the Great Illusion. This chapter will also help you identify if you need outside help.

In addition to the technique for releasing destructive shame, five additional important spiritual tools for creating sexual enlightenment are presented in this book: Breath of Life (Chapter 5), Merge Sexual Energy with Love Energy (Chapter 10), Conscious Touch (Chapter 12), Merge Sexual Energy with Divine Energy (Chapter 14), and Full Body Expanded Pleasure (Chapter 15).

MASTURBATION VERSUS TRANSMUTATION

While masturbation and transmutation both involve the use of sexual energy, they are profoundly different and shouldn't be confused. Therefore, a clarification is important.

Masturbation—a sexual experience resulting from the use of impersonal, primal sexual energy—can be a highly pleasurable experience. It is also a form of spiritually unprotected sex and a practice that can lead to sexual obsession, sexual addiction, and other serious problems. Masturbation—a sexual technique—reinforces the consciousness of separateness.

On the other hand, transmutation—a spiritual tool—reinforces the consciousness of wholeness. This spiritual experience is created by merging primal sexual energy with divine energy by self-pleasuring and praying or meditating. The highly pleasurable experience that can lead to spiritual ecstasy, inspiration, and personal revelation is spiritually protected sex because of the conscious relationship with deity. Therefore, the experience can never lead to sexual obsession, sexual addiction, or other serious problems. Furthermore, the spiritual tool is more effective than any other approach for releasing people from sexual obsession and addiction.

How to Use This Book

The subject of sexuality may be as emotionally loaded for you as it is for nearly every human being on the planet. However, your experiences and behaviors are determined and governed by the unique perceptions, intuitions, feelings, beliefs, and judgments contained in your internal frame of reference. For that reason, it is important for you to feel and think about the significance of the material, to personalize what you read, and to discover and articulate your truth. Only you can create your journey to sexual enlightenment.

As you travel the path, your knowledge may be deepened and extended by turning inward for information and identifying ideas and experiences that up until now have remained out of your conscious reach. With this in mind, you will find sections labelled "For Your Consideration" throughout this book. These sections are designed to assist you with your process of discovery. In addition, it is highly recommended that you record your thoughts and feelings in a personal journal. Fragile, new insights and epiphanies can disappear as quickly as they come to light, so it is important to capture them on paper while they are birthing in you.

The *For Your Consideration* sections have been interwoven with corresponding subject matter to help you fully integrate the material at a deep and personal level. If you come upon one of these sections and feel you have not had enough time to fully process the information it pertains to or you do not want to interrupt what you are feeling and thinking, refer back to the skipped section at a later time—for instance, when you finish reading the chapter.

There are many ways to read and study this book. You may want to study alone, allowing your feelings and thoughts to emerge in privacy. Perhaps you would prefer sharing the experience with your beloved partner, spouse, or close friend. On the other hand, reading and discussing the material in small groups is an intriguing possibility. Together, parents and teenagers might enjoy discovering the new concepts and suggestions found in this book. Ultimately, the decision is yours.

Nevertheless, before you begin to read and study, I strongly suggest you identify specific activities that will help you expand possibilities and find clarity as you relate to new ideas and feelings. For example, when you need to relax and nurture your body, mind, and spirit, what do you do? Are you drawn to poetry and literature, artwork and photography, or various forms of music and dance? In a similar way, embracing the beauty and pleasure of the human body and Earth's nature may inspire and nurture you. Perhaps you might choose descriptions, dialogues, journals, and other personal documents to help you expand your consciousness. Surely prayer, meditation, chants, and sacred rituals are strong possibilities. Hopefully, sexual expressions will be a great tool for you!

Using the suggestions listed in this book or activities of your own choosing, please pinpoint your personal tools for transforming and illuminating your inner path, and then be prepared to use them as you consider the contents of this book. Be courageous and imaginative, but be certain—there will be times when the material clearly demands your highly creative and committed attention! Trust your learning style. Honor and speak your personal truth because your insights and efforts are needed to create a new world vision for present and future generations.

SHARING PERSONAL STORIES

Without a doubt, sharing suitable personal stories is something everyone does, and hopefully, those who hear the tales are inspired and uplifted. The same is true of sharing suitable personal stories about sexuality—they can also be inspiring and uplifting. Furthermore, doing so is necessary for the human race to evolve! We must no longer be silent. Stories can awaken us and illuminate darkness. Sadly, though, most people rarely hear appropriate stories about sexuality.

However, I am humble and grateful to report that my experiences are different. During the last 14 years, I have listened to thousands of extremely brave clients tell me their painfully personal, unique stories about sexuality. Sometimes, the stories are delightfully hopeful and healthy, and other times the stories are frustrating and sad. Nevertheless, I honor and protect all of them. These private, individual stories about sexuality do not and will not appear in this book or any other works of mine—they are not my stories to share. I can and will, however, humbly offer glimpses into my complex and rewarding journey. When possible, appropriate, and helpful, I will also share personal insights gleaned from common threads of information about groups of people. Though their individual stories will remain a mystery, the hauntingly beautiful, tender, and inspiring experiences they have shared are embodied in every word of this book. Therefore, as you begin your journey to sexual enlightenment, know that you are not traveling alone. The many people who have previously journeyed down this path are speaking to you through this book, encouraging and supporting you in your astonishing and rewarding quest.

Since the entire story of my personal journey to enlightened sexuality would fill the pages of a book much larger than this one, I have chosen only a few themes from my academic research and three decades of journals. The selected themes are meant to illustrate and expand concepts about sexuality and spirituality. Please understand, my journey is not a guide, nor is it a model of a path that should or shouldn't be followed. It is simply one person's story. Nevertheless, my tender, erotic, lifelong journey toward and struggle for the truth of my sexuality is deeply spiritual and mystical, graciously creative, and tragically destructive—just like the potentiality of birth, death, and sexuality.

It is my prayer that this book will help you explore, create, and share the story of your journey toward discovering the truth of your sexuality. You and every person on Earth can choose to honor the body, to develop healthy sexual awareness, expression, maturity, and enlightenment. Just as every person is unique, every person's voyage is unique. Your personal path—the sacred celebrations of your life—depends on many circumstances, but especially on your intellectual and emotional freedom as well as your spiritual and religious choices and practices. Hopefully, you will feel free to share your story in appropriate ways and with people who will honor you.

For Your Consideration: Every person alive has a story about his or her sexuality. Have you heard any sincerely shared stories? How did you feel and what did you think? Use your tools for transformation to help open your mind and heart so you can recognize the truth of your story.

PERSONAL QUALITIES FOR FACILITATING SUCCESS

Sexual enlightenment is a powerful, healthy, shame-free, and enlivened state of consciousness based on a deliberate, focused relationship with divinely created energy. By relating to the source, nature, and nine natural gifts of sexual energy, you can consciously unite with the miraculous energy that is in you and throughout the cosmos. Furthermore, this book will teach you eight enlightened expressions of the energy of life—your sexual energy. Hence, you can become marvelously empowered as you learn to transmute the energy of life to create pleasure, love, peace, and goodness in the world.

To ensure your success and, therefore, avoid pitfalls along the way, you should be prepared to utilize certain refined attitudes and states of good will and grace. Because your relationship with your sexuality is a metaphor for your relationship with life, you will be exploring great secrets of life. Moreover, your deepest, fullest dreams for yourself, your family, your friends, and the world will be acknowledged and nurtured as you travel. Since the path is definitely surprising and unusual, consider the following surprising and unusual story that exemplifies important personal qualities needed for you and the world to emerge out of darkness and sexual confusion.

One summer long ago, I went hiking near my home, which overlooks a beautiful, high, red desert, mountainous area near Zion National Park. The sky was blue, the rocks red, and my spirit full. My senses were hyperactive; I couldn't get enough of the beauty and intrigue. I was also aware of the warnings I received from several people about rattlesnakes in the area. I continued in this enchanted state as I walked.

Fifteen minutes later, I suddenly heard a sound, the power of which caused me to leap into the air and turn in the opposite direction. While suspended in time and space, I learned that a rattlesnake was speaking; instinct screamed that I was too close to danger. As my two feet landed on the sand, I hollered loudly and propelled myself away from the sound. Realizing that I was not hurt, I looked around for the snake. It was coiled and silently facing me from a safe distance of a few feet.

What happened next is an experience that dominated my awareness, and to this day, I continue to feel deeply touched and honored to have received such a gift.

I stood motionless as I felt fear subside and elation begin to stir. Overcome and inspired by the presence of the powerful being, I knelt down, breathing deeply and fully. I became aware of the size and length of the snake, paying particular attention to the beige rattles and muted diamonds. Then, I realized we were looking directly and intensely into each other's eyes. As a result of the synergy, my heart and chest began to swell and pulsate. I could feel my consciousness expanding. I recognized the sacred life energy of love as it continued to swell, surrounding Snake and me. Tears filled my eyes as I began to speak gently to her.

"Go away, my friend. Go away," I pleaded. "They will kill you if they find you so close to humans. Go away, my beautiful friend. Go! Go!" Snake watched without moving as I continued to speak to her for several minutes. Captured by the power and beauty of my experience and feeling my consciousness continue to expand, I began to chant. The words were not in English nor were they in any language that humans would recognize. Rather, through ecstasy, the sounds seemed to serve as common ground — a vehicle for sacred communion between Snake and me.

Through my chanting music, I thanked her for allowing me to see her and for not hurting me. I thanked her for staying with me. As I honored her wildness, I remembered mine. Through her rattling music, she opened my heart and kissed the loneliness of my species. She led me to an ancient place that most in my culture have forgotten, a place that acknowledges the oneness of all Earth's beings.

As I stopped singing, she began to dance. Ever so slowly, she began to lift her proud head. Not knowing what she was going to do, I became breathless. Inch by inch and oh so slowly, she began to uncoil her long body with a grace I had never seen. As if reliving and honoring the timelessness of our common ancestry, as if acknowledging my love, her slow-motion magnificence glided across the sand, and in time, quietly disappeared into the arms of the bushes. I was stunned. I was speechless. Only silence remained.

Since our meeting, I have gone back to the place where we came to know each other, hoping to find our beauty, and in some ways wanting to see her again.

She wasn't there; I am never to see her again. I can only hope that she is safe, miles away. I want to believe that she listened to me, that she understood. My life has changed since we met. I feel her all around me. I know you are there, Snake. You have come to me in several forms since then. Humans name you Pink Coachwhip, Diamondback Rattle, Garter Snake, King Snake. I call you friend and teacher.

You share your strength and suppleness with me. My backbone becomes stronger because of you. I learn how you honor (without hesitation), who you are, what you need, and how you give. Because of you, I gain more courage to do the same. The need for freedom to explore is at the center of your world—and mine. May we travel in peace and wonder my friend.

—An Excerpt from the Author's Journal

Naturally, to become sexually enlightened you do not need to have an experience with a snake such as the one described above. Certainly, you don't need to do anything that you believe is dangerous or goes against your safe, personal boundaries. However, what you do need to successfully enter the gates of expanded consciousness and transform your limiting beliefs and actions is a willingness to be open to change. Hopefully, you will embrace the following traits and qualities as exemplified in the story about Snake:

• Be present and conscious in the moment.

• Have faith in the goodness and possibilities of life.

- Acknowledge fear, release it, and open up to love.

- Embrace and honor the common ground of all beings.

- Believe in your ecstasy.

- Freely express appreciation.

- Witness and acknowledge daily miracles.

- Be humble, open-minded, and teachable.

For Your Consideration: Because the subject of this book is sexuality, your response to the material will most likely not be neutral! Therefore, read this book at a time when you can carefully relate to the ideas and use your tools for shifting consciousness. Breathe well and allow new feelings to gently seep into your safe heart as Earth's waters quietly seep into your underground rivers. You are beginning an adventurous journey into expanded consciousness. Designate a notebook or journal for recording your thoughts and feelings as you navigate new possibilities. Keep the material private and safe. Your recorded experiences may be inspiring evidence that you are awakening.

And now as you begin your journey, only make room for truth.

.❧ 1 ❧.
THE MYSTERY CALLS

*W*hat is the source of the mysterious feeling in the body that can be so exciting, pleasurable, and erotic that it ecstatically leads us into another's body, into life? What is the indescribable intensity that can race through the body and cause a person to do anything to experience it, or perhaps anything not to experience it?

We can't touch it. We can't hold it. But, we can feel it. We can watch its intense expression in ourselves or another, but we can't see it. We can want to taste the human body when the mystery is racing inside, but we can't taste the mystery. We can certainly hear the sounds of passion and pleasure, but we can't hear the demanding force. We may not know how to find it when it is lost or lose it when we have found it.

What is the seductive call of the wild and wonderful experience that we secretly ponder yet rarely discuss? Where does it come from? Why is its expression so powerful that it can create or destroy a relationship, a life? We are told that it is good, yet warned that it is bad.

Why are we thrilled by it? Why are we frightened by it? Why are we confused by it? Why do we hate it? Why do we love it? Our sexuality certainly is an enigma!

UNCONSCIOUS, UNEDUCATED, CONFUSED

Sexuality is an enigma for many reasons. Throughout the world, most humans do not know how to talk comfortably about it, or perhaps don't even want to talk about it. Why? Because they are confused. They don't fully understand how to use the mighty force. They don't understand its power because they don't fully understand its natural gifts. And they don't understand its natural gifts because they don't understand its source and nature. Unfortunately (and tragically), this continual confusion and ignorance creates unconsciousness. We live in the sexual dark ages. Where is the light?

Typically, leaders in cultures around the world offer little inspired information regarding sexuality. Spiritual and religious leaders often counsel others about the personal and touchy subject of sexuality. However, they usually only tell us what we shouldn't do. Most Western physicians offer pills, apparatuses, or surgery for dysfunction, but little understanding as to the cause of our concerns. Finding a health professional that discusses sexuality with ease and understanding can be difficult. The Internet and other media offer a look at impersonal sex, or pornography, that may temporarily provide some relief for our need to better understand or experience sexual feelings, but the repercussions can be devastating: shame, guilt, disease, sexual addiction, broken trust, lost income, shattered relationships, and/or death.

THE MIRROR OFFERS REFLECTION

Is there a way to explore our sexual consciousness in a safe and honorable way? Yes, there is. Begin by creating a reflection, a way to look at the mystery. With a mirror, we can obtain a clear reflection of what we look like because our physical image is reflected back to us. This enables us to make better decisions about what we may want to change about our appearance or keep the same.

In keeping with this, we need to create a mirror for viewing our sexuality. A mirror makes it possible to closely examine our sexuality so we can gain an understanding of the relationship we have with our sexual energy. When this understanding is reflected back to us, it creates consciousness.

Generally, there are very few opportunities for us to examine our sexual reflection. Our thoughts most often go unexpressed. Our concerns and dreams about sexuality are usually not shared. Our issues are not addressed. Typically, discussions about sexuality with a partner, friend, parent, or child become awkward and quickly die. Our thoughts are not reflected back to us. They are not witnessed.

For Your Consideration: If your deepest thoughts and feelings about your sexuality were witnessed in a private, safe discussion, what would you share? Would the topic of religion be part of your story? With whom would you share your thoughts and feelings? Would this be the first time you talked frankly about your sexuality?

An excellent way to deepen the understanding of an idea or to affirm a goal is to make it more conscious through the discussion and exploration of possibilities. Amazing things can happen once we do that.

The exploration of space travel is a great example. Goals to explore outer space were made public. This caused an explosion in scientific and technological research. As a result, the goals were met and a fascinating picture of magnificent Earth was taken from outer space and made available for all to see. Earth's picture significantly changed the human consciousness of who we are and where we live by empowering us to see our home clearly—to produce a mirror of understanding for our planet, Earth. Now, we know what our miraculous home looks like in its fullness, which helps us better understand our heavenly home. Therefore, it awakens us to our cosmic role and membership. The magnificence of who we are is reflected back to us.

The same reflection is possible with our sexuality. At this critical time in the world, it is important for humans to increase their understanding of sexual energy, to explore its inner spiritual meaning, and to create a conscious understanding of its nature, source, and natural gifts. The mirror allows us to see—to perceive our curiosity and excitement, our confusion and discomfort. It allows us to stand tall and begin to claim our sexual health and wholeness so we no longer perpetuate misunderstandings, repression, fear, guilt, anger, violence, addictions, broken marriages, and death.

WITNESS THE ENIGMA

This book is intended to become your personal mirror—to offer a reflection that enables you to create a new vision. Hold up the mirror and allow the truth of the mysterious enigma to be heard and witnessed. The mystery of your sexuality is calling to you. It is asking you to suspend, if only momentarily, your disbelief and discomfort in order to entertain new ideas and possibilities, to be creative and courageous in your exploration. It is asking you to use your imagination and the gift of intuition that flows through you. The power of this gift is ignited through the breath—the womb of intuition and deep knowing. Imprisoned ideas and ignorance cannot live in the breath. The breath of life offers a spaciousness of brilliance and freedom that is impossible to define. You are asked to hold up the mirror, to breathe deeply, and to allow the fullness of your brilliance to ask the question: What is the source of sexual energy?

As you allow the breath to expand your mind, you may find that answers to questions about the source of sexual energy dwell in the same mysterious realm as answers to other questions humans courageously ask: Who am I? What is the purpose of my life? What is love? What is death? Is there life after death? Is there a God? What is God? Personal questions and answers like these have been asked and debated since the birth of human consciousness.

When humans ask these questions, they wonder, or even doubt, if they will know the answers with certainty; however, they still strive for understanding. It is the burning curiosity and will to know and live in the seemingly constant face of uncertainty that is the absolute magnificence of the human spirit. The burning desire to know and understand expresses itself in varying degrees in every human being. It requires people to have enduring faith in the continuing gift of life. Each person on this grand Earth listens to and responds to the call of the mystery in his or her own unique way.

Relating to and having faith in the mystery of life requires us to acknowledge that we are part of something greater than ourselves.

Therefore, in order to find peace and love, humans are drawn to spiritual development. They open their minds and hearts to the great mystery of life, to the divine. It is the right and responsibility of each person to take the journey into spirituality.

Throughout the ages of human existence, there have been countless names created to identify the nameless: Mystery of Life, Universal Intelligence, Spirit, God, Goddess, Universal Mind, Shakti, Shiva, Universal Light, Heavenly Mother, Heavenly Father, Great Void, Allah, Buddha, Great Spirit, Higher Self, Higher Power, and so forth. The activity of spiritual awareness—the expression of appreciation and devotion to sacred life and the divine—gives any human being in the world the intellectual and emotional freedom to be open to new ideas about sexuality.

For Your Consideration: Do you believe in a higher power? If so, what is the nature of the relationship?

Do your spiritual beliefs give you the intellectual and emotional freedom to explore old and new ideas about sexuality? Why or why not? Do you agree that an intimate relationship with healthy sexuality includes a conscious relationship with spirituality?

Times are changing quickly. There are many things happening in the world that are truly uplifting and inspiring. But there are also many things happening that are deeply confusing and destructive. It seems there is opposition in all things.

The opposing forces in sexuality are certainly becoming more obvious. Negative, destructive, and dishonoring sexual drives and explorations are increasingly being flaunted through sources such as television, publications, and especially the Internet, which offers seemingly uncensored and unlimited information and resources to the world. Through the Internet, we have access to the collective human mind right at our fingertips. This astounding technological tool offers humans the opportunity to give and receive nearly any kind of information desired. However, the information it offers may or may not be accurate. It also can be constructive or destructive. Thus, it is always important to remember that the Internet is a neutral tool—it has no conscience, so to speak. Therefore, it is wise to be discriminatory in its use.

Through the Internet and other sources, we have the opportunity to learn about topics that have always fascinated us. We get to hold up the mirror. However, these sources have also been used to create the world's mirror for understanding the impersonal, negative, and destructive side of sexuality. This negative vision of sexuality is creating a critical need for discussing sexuality in general. Therefore, there is a bright side!

Now more than ever we have the opportunity and responsibility to create new ideas, ideals, and expressions of sexuality. Because of our exposure to the negative side of sexuality, we can begin to be more aware of sexuality in general and to explore and talk about the positive side of it as well. We can create and hold up the mirror in order to reveal the opposing view of negative sexuality. We have the opportunity and freedom to become more conscious, educated, and enlightened regarding positive expressions, drives, and explorations of sexuality. It is an exciting and awesome phenomenon that is not only a gift and an opportunity, but also our universal responsibility.

UNDERSTAND THE NATURE, SOURCE, AND NATURAL GIFTS OF SEXUAL ENERGY

How do you become more conscious and educated about positive expressions of sexuality? Perhaps, you begin by allowing yourself to be as bold and relentless in creating a positive mirror as those who are responsible for creating the negative mirror. But, there is a major difference: You call upon the best leader possible. The stakes are very high—the lives of those you love. You ask for and receive divine guidance in awakening sexual enlightenment. In doing so, you start to explore the spiritual side of sexuality.

Once again, breathe and allow your imagination to expand a little more on this subject. Science has taught people about the biological component of sexuality. But is it possible that sexual energy or sexual feelings are more than just biological processes? Is it possible that they are something else as well? If you elevate sexuality to the highest level, you entertain the possibility that sexual feelings are spiritually based and, therefore, related to the divine. You may believe that your life force is a gift from the divine, no matter how you personally define the divine. Can you open your mind and heart to consider the possibility that the sexual feelings and drives you feel in your body are actually the sensations of that gift flowing through you? Can you seriously consider the possibility that the source of sexual energy is divine? Yes, you can.

What else could it be? Most religions and spiritual traditions claim we are spiritual beings living in physical bodies. We have inherited our bodies and our spirits from the divine creator of life. Most people believe there is no separation of the spiritual body and physical body until death. What we do with the gift of life in the form of a union of the physical body and spiritual body is our responsibility. Yes, this precious gift is free, miraculous, and from the divine, yet we have been given the opportunity and responsibility to shape and design the use of this life force.

In this context, our life force is neutral in its application. We get to choose how we express it. Thus, wouldn't the same be true for sexual energy? Sexual energy is part of the life force that flows through us. It is a direct manifestation of that powerful force. Therefore, the nature and source of sexual energy is no longer a mystery! The source of sexual energy is divine. Sexual energy is like the technological tool we call the Internet; its nature is impersonal and neutral. In that sense, it has no conscience. Therefore, sexual energy is the impersonal, neutral, and divinely created gift of life that freely flows in everything on Earth and throughout the cosmos.

For Your Consideration: What is your response to the possibility that the pleasure you might feel in your genitals is part of the divinely created energy flowing through your body and everything in the cosmos? Take slow, deep breaths for several minutes and imagine the divine energy flowing through you and the mysterious cosmos. Use your tools for transformation to help you feel your inner and outer mystery.

For the sake of exploration, let's now assume two things: (1) the source of sexual energy is divine, and (2) sexual energy is a neutral life force that you are responsible for learning how to express. Let's assume that when you are feeling sexual energy in the physical body, you are also feeling the power of the gift of life that resides in the spiritual body. You can explore the possibilities and watch what happens. You can question possibilities, make assumptions, and have faith. You can pray, meditate, commune, or ask for guidance and truth. In doing so, you can begin a new and fascinating journey.

You begin the journey by asking the question: If sexual energy is a neutral life force by nature and its source is divine, then what are the purposes, or natural gifts, of sexual energy?

Your responses to the following ideas may not be neutral. Breathe deeply to expand possibilities. Remember, you are considering ideas that can help you create profound sexual health and enlightenment for yourself and for humans everywhere.

Nine natural gifts of sexual energy help us:

1. Relate Generally to Divinely Created Energy. Divinely created neutral life energy is present everywhere in the cosmos; therefore, it flows through us. Earth, our constant companion, is our primal teacher because divine energy creates the sensuous, creative, and powerful nature of Earth that helps us honor our own bodies and energies. Earth's nature constitutes the schoolroom of higher learning for sexuality; we learn to feel life energy through our experiences with Earth. Ideally, we learn to love, nurture, beautify, and strengthen the body and its energy as a vehicle for sexual expression, for living life.

2. Relate Directly to Divinely Created Energy. Our genitals allow us to easily feel the neutral life force available everywhere in the cosmos. Sexual energy certainly gets our attention! Ideally, when we experience sexual feelings, we gratefully claim the gift and inheritance from the divine. We also remember that we are grand spiritual beings whose essence runs through and around our physical bodies.

3. Consciously Unite Primal Sexual Energy with Divine Energy. First, we learn to relate the energy we feel in our genitals with the energy of love. Next, we learn to consciously unite our sexual feelings with our spiritual feelings for the divine. In other words, through sexual energy, we unite our consciousness with divine life energy—God. Ideally, this kind of sexual experience becomes a very powerful form of communion and prayer.

4. Be Responsible for Choices. The sexual energy we feel in the physical body is a result of our direct experiences with the neutral, primal energy of life. Furthermore, powerful sexual feelings demand that we explore and take responsibility for the personal choices we make about how we use this profound energy. Therefore, sexual feelings call to us in powerful, direct voices. They say: "Hello! God is here! You are alive! Feel your life! What choices will you make? Do not be afraid of the brilliant power and creative potential that you feel, but learn to understand and respect it in order to transform your life!"

5. Honor Gender. When healthy sexual energy begins to flow, a consciousness of gender is deepened and we begin to desire sexual expressions with a partner. Healthy and appropriate sexual expressions between partners necessitate an understanding of individual differences and preferences. This, in turn, leads to a conscious relationship with gender and the masculine and feminine energies within and between people. Ideally, the Divine Masculine and Divine Feminine are our perfect models for understanding gender.

6. Create and Sustain a Pure Energy Core. Because we know how to unite neutral life force with our consciousness of divine energy, we can use the transmuted sexual energy to keep the energy core clean and flowing up and down the body—free from the stress and negativity of the human world. Ideally, we can relate well to our unique, natural energy essence of masculine and feminine. We know our energy core is the exclusive home of the Divine Feminine and Divine Masculine within us, and that these divine energies provide us with the inner strength and wisdom to relate to the human world.

7. Enjoy Sexual Pleasure. Sexual energy helps us enjoy the pleasures of being alive in the body on magnificent Earth! And gratefully, the body, or tabernacle, is a sensuous vehicle for expressing sexual ecstasy. Ideally, we learn to enjoy these sacred experiences appropriately when we embrace the nature, source, and natural gifts of sexual energy. Consequently, sexual intimacy is healthy for the body, mind, and spirit.

8. Transform the Earth. Sexual energy is felt and consciously transported in the energy core in order to open our minds, bodies, emotions, and spirits as fully and deeply as possible. Transmuted sexual energy creates the focus, passion, and inspiration that are manifested in the creative and inspired minds of men and women around the world. It is responsible for facilitating the desire and commitment in caring human beings to give gifts to the world and

Earth. Transmuted sexual energy is used to fulfill our purposes and deepest dreams in life and to enable us to become creative geniuses.

9. Procreate. The powerful, creative force of love and divine eternal life that appropriate, mature, and committed partners feel when they express themselves sexually helps them create new life. In doing so, they co-create with the divine.

For Your Consideration: How do you feel in your body? Are you breathing slowly and deeply? What are your initial responses to each of the nine natural gifts of sexual energy? Use your tools for expanding consciousness to help you become more aware. Write your responses to the questions in your journal. If your responses are negative and you feel distressed, please carefully read Chapter 4: Shame—The Great Illusion. The journey into your hidden, inner life may be dangerous if you fail to recognize mirages and illusions.

When you feel the power of neutral life force—sexual energy—and relate to it as divine energy, it enables you to glimpse the creative abilities of God. Therefore, it is inspiring to understand and remember that sexual energy is the energetic entrance into the land of magnificence that is the union of the physical and spiritual bodies. It is the door to a magnificent mansion that has many rooms. The gifts of passion, pleasure, and ecstasy are just the entrance to your sacred home! Think of sexual passion as a wild and wonderful doorbell! If you are afraid to ring the bell, touch the door, or open the door, or equally as important, if you become fixated on the door only and remain ignorant to the fact that the door leads you to holiness and astounding possibilities, you deny yourself astounding blessings! Thus, it is important to learn to relate to your sexual energy correctly and consciously, with sensuous joy and courage.

Though humans may live in the dark, you can be full of light. You can talk about sexuality in a new and different way to your children, teenagers, friends, partners, and spouses. You can share and discuss the true nature, source, and natural gifts of sexual energy. You can be willing to acknowledge that when you feel sexual energy, it is a very direct and powerful experience of astounding divine life. You can learn about sexuality and be willing to talk about it in the same sentence you use to talk about your personal deity. Ideally, you can learn to transport and transmute this amazing energy to help you give and receive the gifts and blessings of love and life.

‿❧ 2 ☙‿

THE ENERGY ESSENCE

*W*hen we claim the divine source and natural gifts of sexual energy, sexuality is no longer a mystery. Relating sexual energy to God and to God's gift of life helps us better understand our sexuality. Therefore, the divine gift of life calls to tell us who we are.

Who are we? We are human beings with varied spiritual and religious traditions, and, generally, we believe we are divinely created—that divine energy pulses through and around us. Most of us agree we have inherited both a spiritual and a physical body from our creator. Well aware that we are gendered beings—male and female—many of us believe in individual male and female deities, in gods who are a union of masculine and feminine qualities, or in a universal higher consciousness that contains masculine and feminine characteristics. Regardless of our different beliefs and the countless names we have created for our personal or impersonal gods, they are our spiritual models of the Divine Masculine and Divine Feminine. Therefore, gender is related to the spiritual nature of sexuality.

As we continue our journey to understand the positive and constructive sides of sexuality, the next step is to closely examine the concept of gender. In order to better understand gender, let's continue to explore the idea of energy in the body. Breathe and open your heart and mind to consider new possibilities.

Technology has been developed around the world that detects and measures energy in and around the physical body. Scientists and others measure human energy fields, or human energy bodies, in various ways and for various reasons. For our purpose here, we do not need to go into great scientific descriptions of energy. However, for the purpose of exploring the spiritual side of sexuality, we might imagine that energy in the body is related in some ways to the individual spiritual body, our spiritual essence. We have talked about sexual energy being God's gift of life, and that the nature of this sacred energy is neutral. Let's go further and imagine that this neutral energy becomes particularized when it enters the physical body of a male or female. Then our essence, or spiritual body, uses this neutral life force to support and nurture who we are as unique individuals.

Imagine that in humans, the spiritual body contains an energetic core that runs through the body like a vibrant river, up and down the spine and brain. Imagine that this grand tunnel contains inseparable energies, which we will refer to as masculine energy and feminine energy. (For the purpose of learning and growing, we talk about these energies as though they are separate, but they certainly are not. A person could not be alive if they were separated.)

Each person has his or her own unique configuration of these energies. To better understand sexuality, gender, and, therefore, our personal relationships, it would be necessary for each person to become conscious of the degree to which he or she carries these two particular energies that help support and nurture his or her uniqueness. Imagine that the natural energy core of most women contains considerably more feminine energy than masculine energy, regardless of sexual orientation.

Conversely, the natural essence of most men contains considerably more masculine energy than feminine energy, regardless of sexual orientation. Furthermore, some men naturally carry far more masculine energy than other men. For example, if we were to use percentages to describe these energy cores, we might say that men with a very masculine essence contain 90% masculine and 10% feminine. Other men might naturally carry 80% masculine and 20% feminine or 70% masculine and 30% feminine, and so forth. These same percentages might be true for women in reverse proportions of the feminine to the masculine. Likewise, some women are naturally much more feminine than other women. It would be highly unusual for a person to carry a natural energy essence that is 50% masculine and 50% feminine.[1]

Just as being physically healthy is important, being energetically healthy is also important. Again, compare the energy core to a river. Just as no two rivers in the world are the same, no two energy cores are the same. Ideally, the life force, or water, would steadily and freely flow—it would be clean and pure. However, if the river is blocked, the water cannot flow well. It may become shallow and barely move. When this happens, the living Earth surrounding the river suffers, and if the river dries completely, the land and animals depending on this natural source of life die.

On the other hand, the river may have so much water that it is flooding its banks, destroying everything in its way and making new pathways that may not be natural and balanced. Thus, too much water can be just as destructive as too little. An ideal natural state is healthy for all life. Just as we understand that humans did not create water—it is a gift of life from our Creator—we understand that each river is unique; no two rivers on Earth are the same. This is also true of human beings—each person is unique and special. Therefore, your energetic river of life, or energy core, is unique.

Self-knowledge is important for health and happiness on all levels. For how can you grow and develop if you are not conscious of and honest about your strengths and weaknesses? Likewise, it is important for you to have a good sense of your energy core. This knowledge helps you know who you are—your natural gifts and weaknesses. As you get to know and understand the degree to which you naturally carry masculine and feminine energies, you develop a better understanding of sexuality, gender, and relationships. Ideally, you will know when your personal river of life is flowing well, when it is dry or barely flowing, and when it is flooding out of control. You will know if the nature of the river's water is balanced or unbalanced. With practice and education, you will learn to relate to the subtleness of the energy body—your masculine and feminine energies—as well as to your physical body.

For Your Consideration: What does masculinity mean to you? What does femininity mean to you? Do you have a sense of your unique energy core and its natural configuration of masculine and feminine energies? As we proceed, it will certainly become clearer to you. For now, take some time to hold up your mirror. Regardless of your roles, who are you as a gendered human being? Do not worry if you feel invisible at first; this will change as you continue on your personal journey.

WHAT ARE THE QUALITIES OF ENERGY?

Awakening and coming alive sexually depends on your ability to relate well to the energies in and around your body. Divinely created energy is everywhere. Understanding what the living energy inside you and throughout the cosmos can look like will help you better understand energy and your energy core.

If you could see living energy, you would see colors as diverse as those seen on Earth with the naked eye or in the cosmos with a telescope! Crystalline white light looks and feels as thin as air, and coal black darkness appears as dense as steel. Energy can be as clear and silent as a deep mountain pool or as transformative and elusive as the northern lights. Oftentimes, shapes and figures reveal themselves—familiar or unfamiliar, static or moving.

Your divinely created life force has emotional, mental, and spiritual qualities that are naturally willing to communicate in varying degrees. For example, the energy from another person's body will sometimes communicate through emotions and other physical feelings in your body. At other times, energy may offer pictures, visions, thoughts, and ideas about another person. Every creative adventure with your divine gift is unique, unpredictable, and, oftentimes, nearly unbelievable! But, God's holy gift is certainly real.

The willingness to be received is an inherent quality of energy, regardless of the form it serves—human, rock, river, horse, soil, moon, or the rest of the cosmos. Energy seems to gratefully receive being witnessed by human consciousness in much the same way a person living in a foreign country appreciates finding someone who speaks his or her language. It is this receptiveness that helps create internal healing. Blocked and distressed energy can release when it is recognized and witnessed by a human being. Love and peace seem to be energy's marvelous goal.

In order to help you better understand energy in the body, I offer a personal experience I had while working as an energy medicine practitioner with a client. I am extremely sensitive to energy and am able to see, hear, and feel it. With spiritual guidance, I help to balance, release, restore, or renew the energetic flow in people. I also help people learn to do the same for themselves. I am not in control of where, when, and how it moves or doesn't move, or the degree to which it communicates and reveals itself. God is the higher power in charge. I never fool myself into thinking that I am making the changes and adjustments; otherwise, my privileged life's work would immediately end. In fact, prayer precedes all of the energy work I do with people, animals, and nature. Therefore, I begin each adventure knowing we will be safe, protected, and guided on our journey.

> *I had been spending the summer in a small village in southern France when a gentleman in his late forties came to see me for help with a non-sexual concern. For several days, he had experienced severe pressure in his head and chest. He was weak, unable to work or sleep, and very emotional and tearful. He was frightened and didn't know what was happening; he felt completely "out of control."*
>
> *I could see thick red clouds of energy around his chest and feel energy pulsating up his spine and out through his head, which to me felt like the extreme energy of fear and worry. I asked if he had seen a medical doctor to which he replied affirmatively. Lab tests had been administered, but the results produced no explanation for his condition. Tranquilizers were ordered by the medical doctors, but the patient refused them.*

I acknowledged his fear and courage, explaining that I sensed what he was experiencing and that he was not alone. I didn't understand his language well enough to have a long conversation, and I imagined that since he didn't know me, he might not necessarily want to talk about personal issues. Therefore, I needed to find a better way for us to communicate than through the spoken word.

On the coffee table was a basket full of my collection of nearly 50 beautifully hand painted wooden eggs from various places in the world. They silently spoke to me, requesting to be a "vehicle for his burdens." Consequently, I asked him to allow each egg to silently carry one of his thoughts. One by one, he slowly and gently lifted the eggs, projected his thoughts or feelings into them, and set them aside. He said nothing, but occasionally breathed heavily or cried. With only a few eggs left in the basket, he stopped, sighed, and collapsed forward.

I looked at his heart and chest, and could see that the thick red energy cloud had dissipated. I asked him if he had words; he had none. His wife and I each held one of his hands as we led him to the private healing room where we continued the session.

During the intense work, I was relating to the energy in his body as it transformed in shape, color, and intensity. At times, it resembled the flow of a red volcanic river. Other times, dark and thick shapes would appear and disappear. Sometimes, the energetic activity was located in a particular part of his body. Other times, it covered the entire body with various tempos and textures. At various times, the energy felt dense and compacted, light and spacious, or tight and hard. Throughout this, he softly cried and moaned, though I did not physically touch him.

A few minutes later, the energy changed drastically. Peace descended into the room like brilliant, silver snowflakes. Silence soothed us.

I was inspired to get a bowl of warm water, some soap, and a towel. Upon returning, I helped the man off of the massage table and into a chair, then knelt by his side and immediately began to massage and gently wash his left hand. As I did this, I watched with inner vision as a steady stream of dark liquid poured from his hands, and I silently asked Earth to receive it. I massaged and washed his hand until the energy release subsided, then wiped the hand dry and held it for several minutes as a pink light cauterized the wound and enlivened the hand.

I did the same with his other hand. As the energy released, it helped me understand that he had abused his hands in some way, or continually used his hands in ways that were detrimental to his well-being.

After washing his hands, we left the private room and returned to the living room. The physical and emotional symptoms subsided. His energy core returned to a healthy flow because the blocked energy in his hands, head, and chest had been released. Consequently, he was greatly energized and wanted to talk.

Through the help of his wife, he shared how he "prostituted" himself with his hands as he continued to use them in work that was dissatisfying and stressful. He no longer used them in creative outlets and they hurt continually. As the session ended, I suggested that he explore at home new possibilities for his life based on what he had just learned and experienced.

A few days later, I learned that because of the session, he and his wife were making long-range goals for changes in his career and future creative projects.

For me, the expanded states of awareness I experience in sessions with clients and their energies are common experiences, just like visiting with my friends and family are common experiences. For me, "non-ordinary states of awareness," are "ordinary" events—experiences that occur daily in my life. They only become non-ordinary when I try to communicate their reality with other human beings who do not experience or understand them. I remember a time in my life when not being able to accurately talk about them created a hole in my being so chronic that withdrawal from my own species had become a way of life.

—An Excerpt from the Author's Journal

All of my negative feelings changed when I realized other human beings also experience expanded states of awareness, but in their own personal ways and for their own personal reasons. Typically, they also have a difficult time sharing their experiences.

EXPANDED STATES OF AWARENESS

Expanded states of awareness such as mystical experiences, unusual creative insights, psychic awareness, intense dreams, rapture of beauty, and so forth happen in varying degrees to everyone! Usually, we just don't talk about them!

Likewise, we also don't talk about another form of expanded states of awareness—orgasm. An awesome result of sexual orgasm can be great pleasure. Orgasmic energy floods the entire psyche with a nourishing, enlivening, and healing gift of life force. The energy core sings with great power and beauty.

Orgasm is also a profound metaphor for the depth and fullness of life's possibilities. Sexuality, in general, is a great metaphor. How we are in our sexuality is how we are in life. Sexual intercourse is a metaphor for life's longing for itself—it wants to be conscious, ecstatic, and peaceful.

Sexuality is about energy—divinely created energy. To evolve sexually, it is critical that human beings relate to energy with open-mindedness and curiosity. A sexual orgasm is a form of released energy. Released, enlivened energy expands pleasure and love, and creates expanded states of awareness. In turn, expanded states of awareness create rapture, ecstasy, and an evolution of consciousness.

The function of expanded states of awareness—non-ordinary states of consciousness—is to create an energetic and psychological breakthrough, the catalyzing of spiritual awakening and physical healing.[2] The expansion of a person's ordinary perceptions can result in a reorganization of her or his energy field so revelation and healing can take place. The energy core is freely flowing, cleansed, and enlivened!

Unfortunately, the Western scientific worldview usually negates the validity of expanded states of awareness; however, the bias against the non-ordinary states of consciousness is as unthinking as the Native American's belief in them is said to be.[3] Many believe that non-ordinary states of awareness are meaningful and common-place, and that they can be completely integrated into nature-based common reality.[4]

Humans have a natural state of being. It is variously known as "being integrated" and "merging mind, body, and spirit." Taoists understand this state to be the "balance of yin and yang." Dine (Navajo) Indians refer to "standing in the center of the world," while the Lakota (Sioux) Indians speak of "walking in a sacred manner" with Earth, whose power and beauty creates ecstasy.

Ecstasy is an experience of great intensity that involves a turning inward, and is stimulated by contact with some environmental condition. Researchers have reviewed data on hundreds of accounts of mystical states that were experienced by people in ancient and modern times. The state of ecstasy almost always takes place after one has been in contact with something regarded as beautiful, valuable, or both.[5]

Seven qualities usually occur during the ecstasy of mystical experiences: (1) a feeling or sense of unity or identity with all things, (2) a sense of tapping into a kind of objectivity or ultimate reality, (3) a sensation of spacelessness and timelessness, (4) a sense of the presence of sacredness or the divine, (5) feelings of joy or blessedness, (6) a belief that the experience is not capable of being accurately explained in words, and (7) a sense of paradox or of understanding the pull of opposites.[6,7] Mystical experiences usually last no more than half an hour and typically begin with a sense of ego surrender to a higher force or intelligence.

For Your Consideration: Do you believe in mystical experiences? What experiences in your life expanded your consciousness? Were they healthy for you and others?

What unique experiences have shaped your life? Have you shared these experiences with caring individuals? Are there unique experiences in your life that you have discounted? If so, why?

෴

What does it mean to be a visible human being? Can others know you if they can't see you clearly? Can you know others if you can't see them clearly?

෴

Being free and willing to open up to wildly transforming mystical experiences gives you the freedom and willingness to open up to wildly transforming sexual experiences. Creating a union between the two is wholeness. It is your conscious power of the divine within you. Do you agree with the above statement? Why or why not?

⟿ ———————————————————————— ⟾

Expressing yourself sexually can expand your consciousness. Sexual experiences can be mystical experiences. Beauty and rapture are born with orgasm. The energy body and physical body can be enlivened and cleansed. The natural receptiveness of your life energy longs to consciously merge with all sacred, divine life.

Expect your normal life to include states of expanded awareness, rapture, and mystical experiences. Why? Because you are more than you think you can be—you are brilliant, loving, open, conscious, powerful, caring, and erotic. You have the ability to be rapturously orgasmic with life! You have divinely created energy flowing through you!

Remember, sexual intercourse and orgasms are metaphors for being fully expressive and alive! Sexuality is potentially the greatest teacher and transformer. If you can't have sexual intercourse physically, perhaps you were meant to have intercourse in other ways. Have intercourse with beauty or with strength and honorability. Have intercourse with fear or love. Have intercourse with birth and death. Only you would know the path.

For Your Consideration: Your sacred, tender, orgasmic heart longs to receive and be filled with the deepest and fullest of life's possibilities. What is it waiting to hear you say? Are you willing to allow your heart's mystical dreams and visions to be impregnated and born?

Notes: Chapter 2 — The Energy Essence

[1] Deida, *Intimate Communion*, 1995.

[2] Grof, *The Adventure of Self-Discovery*, 1988.

[3] Allen, *The Sacred Hoop: A Contemporary Indian Perspective on American Indian Literature*, 1983.

[4] Glendinning, *My Name Is Chellis & I'm in Recovery from Western Civilization*, 1994.

[5] Laski, *Ecstasy: A Study of Some Secular and Religious Experiences*, 1962.

[6] Stace, *Mysticism and Philosophy*, 1960.

[7] James, *Varieties of Religious Experience*, 1902.

✴ 3 ✴

MASCULINE AND FEMININE ENERGY FLOW

*F*or the sake of better understanding masculine and feminine energies—and therefore gender, sexuality, and relationships—we must first generalize about men and women. It is important to understand that we are not talking about the generalization of roles that men and women choose. Modern history is teaching us that it is desirable for both men and women to have equal choices and opportunities. Prior to the events that created more freedom for us to choose roles in our lives and before we understood about energy in the body, there was a strong tendency to believe that roles defined men and women, that they were synonymous with gender.

While it is important that men and women have equal opportunities, each gender is naturally different in an energetic and physical sense; therefore, the masculine and feminine energies they carry cause them to relate to the world of choices in different ways. Now that we have more freedom to choose roles rather than believe they were assigned to us, we have the opportunity to more deeply understand and explore the energetic and natural traits of gender separate from the roles that were previously associated with them.

Overall, men have certain energetic qualities that can be generalized universally, as do women. Obviously, no two men or women are alike. However, we can still generalize about the masculine and feminine energetic qualities that each gender carries. With this in mind, consider the following definitions of masculine and feminine energy.

MASCULINE ENERGY: Men typically carry more masculine energy than women. Therefore, universally, men reveal the following qualities in varying degrees: They are focused, directed, and purposive. They are confident in their strength and power, and know they can make things happen in life and the world. The masculine energy in men has a goal or mission to accomplish. The need to release into the world is great and the driving force behind the mission. Competitive when it comes to setting and accomplishing goals, men naturally guide, lead, teach, and protect others. Furthermore, a man's masculine perception and focused energy is drawn to a woman's feminine energetic qualities.

———————————————————

For Your Consideration: Do you agree with the universal masculine energetic qualities of men described above? In general, what do you think and how do you feel about men? Be honest with yourself. Use your tools for transformation to help clarify your feelings and thoughts.

———————————————————

FEMININE ENERGY: Women typically carry more feminine energy than men. Therefore, universally, women reveal the following qualities in varying degrees: They carry the consciousness of beauty and aesthetics, inside and outside. They are aware of and draw relationships to them. Women recognize and relate to the flow of their inner emotions, which helps them recognize how they feel about what is happening in their bodies, the environment, and all life around them. Women are emotionally open and vulnerable in order to receive themselves, others, and life. Therefore, feminine energy is love. The feminine body invites and receives the ideas, focus, and strength of the masculine mind and body.

For Your Consideration: Do you agree with the universal feminine energetic qualities of women described above? In general, what do you think and how do you feel about women? Be honest with yourself. Use your tools for transformation to make your answers crystal clear. Record your feelings and thoughts.

THE RELATIONSHIP OF MASCULINE AND FEMININE ENERGIES

The masculine and feminine energies within and between people form a relationship that creates a flow of energies. It is the flow of these very different energies and qualities that causes humans to be attracted to each other. The relationship of the feminine (physical) and the masculine (consciousness) creates life. Therefore, we can imagine the results of their union to be the cosmos, the Earth, and the human body. The masculine and feminine energies in men and women are drawn to each other, creating sexual interest, the excitement of sexual tension, and the interest in and need for love, human friendship, and relationships. Furthermore, the attraction of energies is true for same sex romantic and sexual relationships.

The relationship of the Divine Masculine and Divine Feminine creates a flow of life that is present everywhere and in everything. Depending on our beliefs, we imagine impersonal or personal deities to be our models for creating sacred life and loving relationships.

In order to better understand the masculine and feminine relationship within and between people, the relationship of the human masculine sperm and feminine egg can be used as an obvious metaphor.

THE SPERM SPEAKS FOR THE MASCULINE: If the sperm speaks for the masculine in men (and women), it can also speak for men in general. It might loudly and firmly say: "Here I am! I am confident in my power and strength. I am focused, directed, and confident. I can create new possibilities, new life." The masculine sperm is drawn to the mystery, warmth, and beauty of the feminine egg, which is many times bigger than it. Consequently, the sperm wants to initiate contact with the egg because it has a goal, a life's purpose of finding and entering into the world of possibilities that the egg represents. The need to release into the world is the great and driving force behind its mission. We can think of the tiny sperm as a miraculously focused energetic idea. Therefore, it shouts to all sperm and anything that will listen: "Let me out of here. I am going to be the first one there!" Then, off it goes—not because it loves the egg, but because it is on a mission and has a life's purpose to fulfill.

THE EGG SPEAKS FOR THE FEMININE: If the egg speaks for the feminine in women (and men), it can also speak for women in general. The egg is waiting to relate and open up to the fullness of life. It wants to be filled with the power and perceptive focus of the masculine sperm. It may be fair to imagine that of all the sperms racing toward it, the egg draws in the energy of one particular sperm because it wants to relate to it, because it is in love with the one it allows to initiate an opening. The egg loves feeling its physical self, its physical aliveness and warmth. It feels radiantly alive. It loves life. It is emotionally alive. It loves the beauty of all life around it. With the mystery of its beauty, warmth, and fullness, it calls to the sperm: "Here I am! Come to me! I am open. I am love. Fill me up with your focus, your consciousness, your guidance, your protection. I want to feel our union, our love, our relationship."

The mutual consent of attraction is like two magnets. Through the relationship of these energies, new creation is possible. Therefore, when the qualities of feminine energy are contained in the feminine physical body, a man generally perceives the woman's body to be about beauty, warmth, soft curves, and the exciting potential of the unknown world of possibilities. When the qualities of masculine energy are contained in the masculine physical body, a woman generally perceives the man's body to be about strength, power, confidence, and protection.

For Your Consideration: As you read about the cycle of masculine and feminine energy flow described below, consider the following questions: Which type of energy do you relate to more easily when you are sexually expressive? Generally, do you prefer to initiate and give pleasure (masculine) or open and receive pleasure (feminine)?

The Cycle of Masculine and Feminine Energy Flow

There is a fascinating flow of masculine and feminine energies that helps create what we know as life within and around us. An understanding of the relationship of these energies is at the center of healthy sexuality. It helps us comprehend who we are as gendered human beings, and therefore, what men and women typically need and want. Generalizing about the energetic qualities of men and women can help us better understand our relationships and ourselves. It can help us comprehend not only the flow of the energies in all types of human relationships, but also in Earth's nature as well as in families, communities, businesses, countries, cultures, planets, and the cosmos!

Consider the following model of the cycle of masculine and feminine energy flow. The model describes energy that is clear, brilliant, and balanced. It describes the flow of energy within and between men and women in a heterosexual relationship. It also describes a masculine and feminine energetic relationship that is healthy, one that is flowing and moving on all levels: physically, emotionally, mentally, spiritually, and sexually.

THE CYCLE OF MASCULINE AND FEMININE ENERGY FLOW

Masculine Initiates

↗   ↘

Feminine Receives   *Feminine Opens*

↖   ↙

Masculine Releases

THE MASCULINE INITIATES: A masculine man is attracted to the energy of a feminine woman because she carries qualities he wants to know and experience. A man is attracted to the ability of a woman to be naturally warm and loving. He perceives the beauty of her body and the way she moves in it. He sees and is attracted to the mystery of her emotions, vulnerability, and openness. He understands that she can be tender, loving, and caring. He has the confidence to initiate contact with her. He focuses his energy and thoughts on her, and he moves toward her.

THE FEMININE OPENS: A feminine woman draws a masculine man into her presence because she feels his confidence, strength, and focus and wants to relate to him. She feels safe in his presence, and therefore, she opens to his potential—she will only open up if she feels safe. When she feels protected, she is willing to allow him to guide the process of relating. She feels him in every way possible. She smells him, hears him, sees him, and opens her heart, mind, and body to him.

THE MASCULINE RELEASES: The masculine man is encouraged by her opening up to him, and so he continues to initiate. Eventually, he wants to release all that he has into the woman. He releases his perceptions and ideas, his physical power, his money, his commitment, his leadership, his willingness to protect and guide her, and finally, his body. He does all of this for a reason: He wants to be received! He wants to be adored! He wants to be loved! He wants to be close to what is inside her heart and body. He wants to release his masculine focus and drive into her warmth and love.

THE FEMININE RECEIVES: The feminine woman receives this man because she loves who he is and feels safe to receive his strength, focus, leadership, and protection. In his presence, she feels especially beautiful—inside and outside. She opens her heart, her emotions, her body, her arms, and her legs because she wants to be filled with him. She wants to relate to and receive him! She adores and loves him! She loves their relationship and wants the cycle of initiating, opening, releasing, and receiving to continue. Because of him, she feels the fullness of possibilities and wants to be filled with their life together.

The energetic flow of life creates the love and peace of union on all levels. The masculine man feels adored and loved. He wants to continue to release all that he has into his partner because he wants to feel fully received. Through the relationship he has with his feminine woman, he is able to release into the depths and fullness of life. Therefore, he wants to continue initiating and releasing his life force into her life, her body, and her love. Doing so is part of his life's purpose.

Being filled with the presence of the man she loves and adores gives the feminine woman a reason to continue with the cycle of opening and receiving. She wants to receive him because it fills her body, heart, emotions, and mind with love. Therefore, she wants the relationship to continue, and she feels safe to open up and receive because she is protected.

Maintaining a healthy flow and attraction of the masculine and feminine energies within and between us is critical. It helps us feel love, comprehend emotional and spiritual truths, and realize our dreams and goals. When we are aware of the energy flow of sacred life, we can watch its flow in the world around us—in Earth's nature, in human nature. Ideally, we witness the wonderful marriage of physical and energetic life forces. We understand how the inseparable union of the two works, and we understand when it doesn't work. We see the physical world around us and know it is full of the gift of life from the divine.

Becoming conscious of the cycle of masculine and feminine energy flow is empowering because it helps us better understand our relationships. Typically, the natural, unique amounts of masculine and feminine energies within a person's energy core are not present in equal quantities. Furthermore, it is important to note that our goal is not to make the quantities equal (i.e., 50% masculine and 50% feminine), as many people would like to believe. Rather, our objective is to learn to equally value feminine and masculine energies because both are equally important! The proper goal is to have a healthy, vibrant flow of the natural, unique configuration of energies within each person. Ideally, it is our uniqueness that we come to understand, honor, and love. Emotional, physical, mental, sexual, and spiritual health is tied to our gender. Women are naturally different from men. Men are naturally different from women. In my work with thousands of men and women, rarely have I met a person with energies that were equal in quantity.

Understanding the descriptions of masculine and feminine energies can help us better understand our personal strengths

and weaknesses, our gender differences, our relationships with people, and our love relationships with men and women. It helps us
understand sexuality, particularly sexual expression, because it is
the attraction of masculine and feminine energies that creates sexual attraction.

---

*For Your Consideration: The cycle of the masculine and
feminine energy flow can be easily remembered if you relate
it to sexual intercourse: initiate (masculine), open (feminine),
release (masculine), and receive (feminine). Take as much
time as you need to integrate and memorize the ideas. Healthy
sexual intercourse is a metaphor for the energetic flow of all
life. Recognizing this truth will free the human race of sexual
ignorance and confusion.*

*Do you understand your natural energetic strengths and weak-
nesses? For example, if you naturally have a small amount of
masculine energy, is it strong and confident or weak and timid?
If you naturally have a small amount of feminine energy, is it
open and receptive or closed and withdrawn?*

*What are the states of the unique energy cores of your partner
and other people in your life to whom you relate? Observe
them with a curious and understanding eye.*

EXAMPLES OF THE UNION OF
MASCULINE AND FEMININE

Regardless of the personal reasons driving our desire to become sexually enlightened, it is vitally important that we have a thorough understanding of the energetic flow of the inseparable masculine and feminine energies within and between people—this is the very foundation of our new sexuality paradigm. Think of the masculine and feminine energies, which flow up and down the center of the body, as being part of a person's unique energetic essence, and therefore, spiritual in relation to personal gods. Wonderful examples of the union of masculine and feminine are inherent in most of the world's spiritual and religious philosophies. Several examples follow.

1. Healthy and spiritual sexual expressions are based on a belief in divinity—the pure and perfect relationship of the Divine Masculine and the Divine Feminine. From this divine relationship, we have received our precious gift of life, the union of the body and the spirit. Therefore, we know we have inherited a spiritual essence whose nature and source is divine, and we strive to honor and protect it as it flows through us. Ideally, our spirituality helps us to know and remember who we are—to keep the river of life pure and clean—so we can learn from and deepen our relationships with the divine.

2. Organized religions and spiritual philosophies are examples of the inseparable flow of masculine and feminine energies. The structure and path of organized religions and philosophies—the principles and doctrines, the guidelines and goals—can be thought of as masculine energetic qualities. But, the masculine structure itself is not enough. Identifying only the masculine structure leaves

us out of touch with the feminine qualities of love, beauty, and emotions. Therefore, the ideal structure of organized religion has a grand purpose and goal. It enables us to learn to embrace the feminine qualities of love, grace, compassion, and inner beauty. Discipline and obedience (masculine) become personal structures that can lead us to peace and love (feminine). The structure (masculine) of the religion protects and guides members into the expression of their deity's grace and love (feminine).

3. Ideally, temples and shrines worldwide are wonderful examples of the perfect union of the inseparable masculine and feminine. The physical structures (masculine) of the sacred sites enable devotees to be safe and protected in their expression of beauty and love. When they enter the physical structures and participate in sacred ceremonies, their experiences provide an understanding and expression of the divine organization (masculine) for receiving particular blessings of love and peace (feminine). Within a temple, it is possible for a spiritual seeker to become conscious of the holy union of divine purpose (masculine) and divine love (feminine).

In summary, the union of masculine and feminine creates a relationship of purpose and love between the body and spirit, the heart and mind, and the physical and energetic. Your energetic essence—your spiritual relationship with the divine—flows up and down throughout your body. Ideally, as you learn and remember who you are, your spirituality will grow and strengthen. You will understand the source and purpose of your life. You will learn to relate with adoration and respect to the powerful spiritual being, Earth, which provides the physical bodies for all beings. You will learn to honor and take care of your body. You will learn to understand and relate to your essence of life—the invisible, unique, and sacred core of energy in your body. It is this pure and magnificent space within you that is home.

———————————————————————

For Your Consideration: Understanding the inner flow of your energy body may take time and certainly requires an open mind. Is your flow of masculine and feminine energies healthy when you are expressing yourself sexually? If not, at what point does it weaken and why does this occur?

Is your partner's flow of masculine and feminine energies healthy when he or she is expressing himself or herself sexually? If not, at what point does it weaken and why does this occur?

Fear, envy, anger, resentment, blame, and any other manifestation of emotional, spiritual, mental, or physical anxiety create stress and an imbalance in the energy core. Prolonged and chronic energetic stress creates a dam in your inner river and is one of the main causes of sexual disinterest and dysfunction. However, being human means you are constantly learning to rebalance your inner energies in order to create harmony. Typically, what stresses you and causes your energy core to be constricted or blocked? Are your responses to the tension healthy? Do you have a sense of what you can do to keep your natural essence flowing and healthy?

———————————————————————

ᴥ 4 ᴥ
SHAME — THE GREAT ILLUSION

*N*ow, it's time to explore ways to put the natural gifts of sexual energy into practice. First, however, it is important to equate impersonal sexual energy with your personal feelings for the divine. This is an idea that some people may find difficult to embrace. Thus, they might say: "How can I possibly relate intense feelings of neutral sexual energy with my personal feelings for God? I find it unacceptable, abnormal, and strange."

Since some people may feel strange about spiritualizing their neutral sexual energy, let's start with what people might believe to be acceptable, normal, and sacred such as temples, shrines, and powerful locations in nature. These sites are typically tributes to the divine where humans can open up to and receive inspiration, blessings, creative power, and peace. They are a source of renewed psychic energy and spiritual revitalization. These holy places become the center of the universe—the contact between heaven and earth—because they are focal points of divine energy.

Preparing to build a healthy foundation for sexual expression includes the process of consecrating the body—to declare and make the body sacred, to devote it irrevocably to a relationship with the divine. Ideally, you learn to venerate the body—to give it reverential respect in the same way you venerate sacred spaces. When you are successful in purifying your body and honoring its sacredness, your body becomes a mobile sacred place, or tabernacle.

If you don't feel good about your body or good about living in it, or if you regret or even abhor how you or someone else has treated it, you may not feel worthy to enter the pure realm of the divine. Negative feelings about your body can be very painful. The implications can be so intense, they may seem impossible to describe. Arguably, there is nothing more destructive to the human mind and spirit than feeling a highly negative sense of shame in the body—to think you are bad to the core; to believe the body is ugly, dirty, and wrong; and to feel a nagging need to hide the body and not be sexually expressive. This kind of thinking is the most powerful tool for imprisoning people in a dark and unconscious relationship with their sexuality. This deadening and dangerous thinking ruins personal health, friendships, partnerships, marriages, and, consequently, families and communities.

However, not all shame is destructive.

CONSTRUCTIVE AND DESTRUCTIVE GUILT AND SHAME

Constructive guilt and shame work hand in hand and are desirable road blocks and red flags in emotionally, mentally, and spiritually healthy human beings. Guilt is awareness (masculine energy) that you have done something wrong or committed a crime, an understanding that your actions are not in alignment with your personal values and morals or those of society. The awareness of guilt is accompanied by feelings (feminine energy) of shame—a negative emotion that combines constriction in the energy body with the feelings of unworthiness, embarrassment, and dishonor. Your masculine energy can help you reassess a situation and redirect your energy into correcting a path of action that caused you guilt and shame, thereby leading you back into self-acceptance and self-love. The constant willingness and commitment of an individual to empower the flow—initiating, opening, releasing, and receiving—of the masculine and feminine energies within creates health and autonomy. The masculine needs the feminine to create awareness (guilt) when it is not on track with its goals. The feminine needs the masculine to direct it out of emotions that can cause energetic constriction (shame) and back into a healthy flow of self-acceptance and self-love in the energy core.

Destructive guilt and shame hurts the body and haunts the heart. It causes the flow of masculine and feminine energies within a person to stop, creating a breeding ground for destruction. The feminine closes and the masculine cannot release into it. The feelings of embarrassment, unworthiness, and dishonor normally released in constructive guilt and shame can no longer be accessed or released. This dammed energy flow creates great mental and physical tension, which multiplies and spreads into various places of the body.

In time, this blocked energy causes you to erroneously—and usually unconsciously—create the belief that the Great Illusion you're experiencing is true and real. Thus, you no longer believe you have done something bad or wrong. Now, you feel you are bad and wrong. The difference is profound and can be catastrophic. For instance, it can cause deeply damaging beliefs: I am ugly. I am pathetic. I am dishonorable. My body is disgusting. Sex is disgusting.

My body stinks. The fluids in my body are filthy. I am evil. My body is evil. My genitals are ugly. I am immoral for wanting oral pleasuring. I am not loveable. I shouldn't be alive. I am not worthy of living. I am bad to the core. I am full of sin. I am useless and weak. I am a failure. I am unworthy of God's love. God hates me.

The haunting effects of destructive shame prevent people from wanting to hold their mirrors high and reveal not only the beauty of the human body and spirit, but also the awakened truth about sexuality. If a person isn't aware of the presence of deep, destructive shame, it doesn't mean he or she isn't affected by it. The feelings may simply be nearly impossible to bear. It is safe to say that most people struggle, in varying degrees, with negative feelings about sexuality at some point in their lives. Furthermore, in teaching and counseling thousands of people, I have learned that shame and rebellion associated with religion and relationships with deities are the major reasons most people have difficulty finding sexual health and fulfillment.

THE METAPHYSICS OF SHAME

Destructive shame is a blocked emotion in the body. But what created the emotion? Energy!

The blocked emotion of destructive shame is a person's response to the energy of human thoughts in the body. When people use the divine gift of life in their energy cores to think, the results are released into the environment. Thus, released energy—thought forms—lives in and around us. New technology is being developed to prove this idea to be true to the disbeliever just as science and technology proved microscopic germs and viruses live in and around the human body. We all know what being around negative, angry, or critical people feels like and we certainly know what being around positive, peaceful, or loving people feels like. When comparing the two situations, most people can become aware of what happens in their bodies—they respond to the energetic thought forms. When you are aware of feelings in your body, you may be able to feel shame in various places and then release the energy.

The greatest and deepest desire of the bodies of all women through out all time—is to be radiantly conscious and joyously free of illusions! Self-love is a celebration of beauty. Sexual intimacy is a celebration of beauty. It is not enough to open her arms and legs and mouth to her lover. Ideally, she will be eager and brave enough to love who she is. She will be ready to crack open the limiting whispers of consciousness, which try to convince her that she is something less than beautiful. Otherwise, if shame is allowed to thrive in her trembling inner thighs, her sex will be quick and unconscious, even if it is orgasmic. The illusion silently creeps into the moist and warm sacred cave, anesthetizing and shrinking its victim as it multiplies. Her sacred cave then becomes her terrorized tomb.

Often, the open window allows friends to approach: the sweet scent of plumeria blossoms, wind dances with palm tree, Gulf of Mexico's blue womb, and conversations of birds. Today, I see sparrow whose nest is above my window. She looks at me directly. Her laser eyes lock onto me, pulling me from my chair, calling me from shame, demanding that I watch as she joins wind. In union, they fly, carrying my blue ribbon of shame, pulling and pulling the cord from my infected heart. Higher, lighter they fly until it worms itself from my chest, dissipating

*and disappearing far above me. Once again, I breathe. I flow. I
am graced. Thank you, my loyal friends—the local healers.*
                              —An Excerpt from the Author's Journal

---

*For Your Consideration: Have any of your responses to ideas
in this book made you feel uneasy, bad, angry, etc.? If so, have
you allowed yourself to take time to let your emotions breathe
and swell? Deepen and expand your knowledge by using your
tools for transformation, such as listening to music, writing, or
meditating, to turn inward for information that until now has
remained out of your conscious reach. You are the only one
who can feel your emotional truth.*

*Every person alive is responsible for being intimate with his
or her inner world. Sexual enlightenment requires emotional
and spiritual freedom. Do you trust your feelings?*

*What is your relationship with your body? With Earth? How do
you feel about nudity? How do you feel when being physically or
sexually intimate? How do you feel when your body is touched
or when touching your partner's body? Are your decisions about
how you express yourself physically or sexually based on personal preferences of what is right for you in your life, or are your
choices based on fear, intimidation, or some other influence?*

What is your relationship with destructive shame? Do you
recognize it or do you suspect it is quietly hiding inside?

⟞⟞⟞ ———————————————————————— ⟞⟞⟞

FIRST SPIRITUAL TOOL — RELEASE THE ENERGY OF SHAME

During private sessions with clients, I have witnessed many people successfully learn and use this spiritual tool — non-orgasmic women, individuals struggling with anger and shame as a result of their sexual orientation or spiritual and religious upbringing, sexually repressed couples, victims of sexual violence and the per-petrators of such tragedies, people preparing for marriage and sexual intimacy, etc.

Hopefully, you are not infected with the illusion of deep shame. Remember, however, that no matter how sexually healthy you are or what your reasons are for reading and studying this book, you are not immune to the effects of destructive shame. It is a potential concern of every person on Earth. On the other hand, if you believe destructive shame is living in you and creating an illusion about who you really are, the following method for releasing shame can be very helpful. Before you start the process, however, read and study the three steps so you thoroughly understand them.

⟞⟞ STEP ONE: Describe aloud how you feel and what you think with short, clear statements: "I feel_____!" Keep it simple — no history, no blame. Simply share your feelings and thoughts. For example: "My head hurts. I can't breathe. My arms are tight. My knees hurt. My chest aches."

Becoming aware of your body's feelings helps you become aware of your subconscious thoughts. For example: "I am bad. I am dishonorable. I am dirty. I stink. I am disgusting. I am pathetic. I am wrong. I am a failure." The list may be long, and it will not be pretty. Allow yourself the time it takes to acknowledge and speak aloud your perceived truths. When you are finished, go to Step Two.

 STEP TWO: Say the following words aloud: "That is shame. It is not me." Repeat the words several times until you clearly remember that who you are in your divine core is separate from the blocked energy in your body that carries the thought forms of shame and negativity. When you become conscious of this reality, the blocked energy in your body gratefully starts to release—it doesn't want to be there any more than you want it to be there! Human thought forms want to be acknowledged and freed by humans. Recognizing shame may be difficult if you have strongly identified it as your inner truth. At first, when you begin the process of releasing, you might think you are fooling yourself.

 STEP THREE: Say your full name clearly and courageously. "I am _____." Claim your true essence. Describe the positive aspects of your personality and life. For example: "I am a loving person. I am a good father/mother. I am a hard worker. I am helpful. I am intelligent. I try my best. My body is beautiful. I appreciate my body." As you acknowledge the truth, be aware of the tension in your body releasing. Be sure you can claim your divine essence and God's love for you before you stop describing yourself.

Beware of any feelings of shame that might remain in the body. If needed, take time to repeat the three steps.

Having a partner observe and assist you can make a big difference. Your partner can remind you of the three steps—encourage you to describe negative thoughts and feelings, claim your name and pure essence, and, finally, describe positive and constructive feelings. Your partner can also remind you to keep descriptions short and simple and to allow time to feel the emotions in your body.

This shame releasing process is excellent to use over and over again until you are conscious of when you are carrying destructive shame so you can quickly release it. With wisdom and commitment, it is possible to release the blocked energy of thought forms. For some people, however, it may take professional help. Nevertheless, you can make the journey under the protection and love of your spiritual teachers.

When I work with clients and use this three-step process, I can see the blocked energy in the body, watch it be released, and know if all of it has been released or not, which can be very helpful. But clearly, this three-step process is possible to learn on your own, and most people are aware of any negative feelings or energies that persist.

So once again, how do you equate the neutral or impersonal feelings of sexual energy with personal, intense feelings of love for the divine? First, you treat the sacred body, the tabernacle for divine energy, with love and respect. Next, you release destructive and blocked shame in order to fully embrace the true nature, source, and natural gifts of sexual energy. Last, you ask for and open up to divine guidance in your sexual expressions. This physical, emotional, mental, and spiritual process evolves naturally over your lifetime, helping you build a foundation for healthy and spiritual expressions of sexual energy one step at a time. As you create sexual enlightenment, you join fellow human beings throughout the world who are doing the same. Your combined efforts create a web of mirrors that reflects sexual truth and light.

For Your Consideration: Remember that the energetic forms of shame may be all around you, depending on your environment and the people with whom you associate. Use your tools for transformation to imagine how energetic thought forms might feel in your body.

What would being buried alive for years or decades feel like? How might shame respond to your loving, liberating energy? How might shame—the Great Illusion—feel if you helped it merge with the energy of peace and love? Create the experience within you.

.@ 5 @.

EIGHT ENLIGHTENED
EXPRESSIONS OF SEXUAL ENERGY

*B*efore we continue on our journey to open the closed doors that prevent awakened expressions of sexuality, let's review what we have considered so far.

We explored the nature and source of sexual energy. We examined the idea that the journey begins when we understand sexual energy is a neutral life force that is a divine gift. Therefore, sexual energy is no longer a mystery! It is easy to comprehend—when we are feeling sexual energy in the body, we are actually feeling divine energy. Our energetic life force runs up and down the center of our bodies like an inner river. This divine energy feeds and enlivens our physical bodies. Knowing these things will help us learn to use our neutral life force to become healthier, happier, and more brilliantly aware and loving.

In addition to exploring the nature and source of sexual energy, we considered nine natural gifts of sexual energy, which help us: (1) relate generally to divinely created energy, (2) relate directly with divinely created energy, (3) consciously unite primal sexual energy with divine energy, (4) be responsible for choices, (5) honor gender, (6) create and sustain a pure energy core, (7) enjoy sexual pleasure, (8) transform the Earth, and (9) procreate.

Now, we are ready to continue on our journey. The eight enlightened expressions of sexual energy will help you create astonishing sexual consciousness by providing powerful tools for transformation in all aspects of your life. Each enlightened expression relates to a different part of your body, which will help you learn and remember them. In addition, this association will help you respect and love your whole body, not just part of it, as a personal vehicle for sexual intimacy.

You will relate differently to each enlightened expression of sexual energy, depending on your age, physical abilities, gender consciousness, physical health, and personal circumstances. Remember, you are a sexual being from the moment you are conceived. You will be a sexual being until you draw your final breath. Every age and stage of your life offers, or perhaps demands, an opportunity for you to relate to specific enlightened expressions.

Though sexual intercourse can be exquisitely pleasurable, it is equally transforming as a metaphor for the flow—initiating, opening, releasing, and receiving—of masculine and feminine energies within and between people. People who never will or no longer can experience sexual intercourse must be wise and not let the memory or lack of memory create profound frustration, longing, or shame. Physical, sexual intercourse and orgasm are only one part of being sexually expressive. A person who has never experienced sexual intercourse and orgasm or who has been sexually celibate for years or even decades has as much opportunity to be a sexually enlightened human being as sexually active men and women.

As we explore the eight enlightened expressions of sexual energy, remember that references to the masculine and feminine energies in men and women do not refer to generalized gender roles—men and women choose roles based on many factors. However, we can generalize about the natural configuration of energies that flows through all men and women. Men have an energetic presence that allows us to generalize about men, and the same is true of women. Therefore, it is possible to say that both men and women have certain qualities that can be generalized universally. Obviously, no two men or women are alike; however, we can still generalize about the masculine and feminine energetic qualities that each gender carries.

Following are brief descriptions of the eight enlightened expressions of sexual energy, which will be discussed at length in subsequent chapters. Please take time to personalize the ideas and think about which enlightened expressions you relate to more. Remember, we are talking about ideal states of consciousness that can be achieved over time as you create a new relationship with sexual energy.

❧ **1. Love the Human Body and the Earth.** The first enlightened expression of sexual energy is symbolized by the pelvic floor area of the body, including the base of the spine, the anus, the thighs, and the legs. We are conscious of our reciprocal relationship with Earth and our appreciation for the sacred life force it provides. We accept and love our physical bodies as we hear, smell, taste, see, and touch the Earth. We embrace, nurture, and protect the whole body, which is a sacred tabernacle for the exploration of sexual expression. We understand and honor our highly charged and primal sexual energy. Though this powerful and earthy energy is impersonal, we express it in a personal, safe, and intimately free way by ourselves or with our sacred lovers. Claiming Earth's mysterious, wild, and beautiful nature as our own healthy nature creates a spiritually and sexually intimate experience.

✑ **2. Honor Gender.** The second enlightened expression of sexual energy is symbolized by the area of the genitals, inside and outside the body. As the divine gift of life passes through the genitals, it is felt as sexual energy more than in any other place in the body! We joyfully accept its nature, source, and natural gifts in our lives. No other place in the body reveals such physical differences between men and women as the genitals. Therefore, healthy sexuality is possible when we sincerely explore, understand, and honor gender differences and the healthy flow of energies between them. In the deepest and fullest sense, we spend our lives becoming increasingly aware of what it truly means to be a man or a woman.

✑ **3. Embrace Healthy Masculine Sexual Energy.** The third enlightened expression of sexual energy is symbolized by the solar plexus—the relatively unprotected area just below the rib cage. Because the masculine energy in men and women offers protection, it is easy to remember the third enlightened expression is about healthy masculine sexual expression and confidence in men and women. Both partners are willing to initiate sensuous touch. Both partners direct and orchestrate sexual pleasure and intimacy. A woman learns about the expression of masculine sexual energy by watching her confident masculine partner and relating to her inner masculine energy.

✑ **4. Embrace Healthy Feminine Sexual Energy.** The fourth enlightened expression of sexual energy is symbolized by the chest, heart, and arms. The heart is a universal symbol of love and emotions, and, therefore, a symbol of the feminine energy in men and women. As natural, impersonal sexual energy is expressed with the consciousness of the feminine in men and women, the sexual experience becomes very personal; there is no separation between the deep emotions of love and the intense sexual energy. A masculine person learns about the expression of feminine sexual energy from his sensitive emotions and feminine partner.

✍ **5. Communicate Sexual Truth.** The fifth enlightened expression of sexual energy is symbolized by the throat area. We are aware of and fully comfortable with communicating our sexual feelings, desires, needs, and emotion, and willingly receive personal sexual truth from our partners. Because our partners know they are responsible for their own pleasure, they can listen to their bodies and communicate their personal needs in positive ways. Love and intimacy are deepened as partners give and receive sexual truth—the acts of giving and receiving are both essential for successful and healthy sexual expressions. We are then prepared to express ourselves with the divine during sexual intimacy.

✍ **6. Witness Sexual Truth.** The sixth enlightened expression of sexual energy is symbolized by the eyes. Partners are deeply aware of what is happening between them because they are constantly looking into each other's eyes. Because they receive passionate and powerful energy from each other's eyes during lovemaking, they witness the vibrant, holy truth of the moment. Furthermore, it is through the eyes, the windows to the soul, that partners share their vulnerability, intimacy, and love, following each other into the freedom of the cosmos and heavens. Thus, healthy spiritual expressions become highly transpersonal and mystical.

✍ **7. Unite Sexual Energy with the Divine.** The seventh enlightened expression of sexual energy is symbolized by the crown of the head. We consciously and simultaneously feel sexual energy and spiritual love. Both are united. The place in the human mind and heart that recognizes the sacred source of sexual energy also opens to God through sexual expressions. Therefore, during sexual intimacy not only is there a feeling of union between the masculine and the feminine within and between committed lovers, but also there is a feeling of union with God—the Divine Masculine and Divine Feminine.

✍ **8. Receive Inspiration and Revelation.** The eighth enlightened expression of sexual energy completes the circle of all the enlightened expressions. It is symbolized by a circle that represents the core of the energy center that pulses through the center of the body from the bottom to the top. We are constantly striving to keep our home, our spiritual center, pure and clear. Depending on our spiritual and religious beliefs, we learn to go home to our center through various ways such as prayer, meditation, love, beauty, or music. We also learn to go to our center through sexual energy. After we have learned to unite sexual energy with feelings of love for God, we learn to use the union to receive personal revelation, guidance, and creative inspiration. Consequently, we transmute sexual energy into focused energetic power to help transform our bodies, the world, and Earth.

✍ ——————————————— ⊙✍

For Your Consideration: How do you feel in your body?
What are you thinking? Are you breathing? Is the illusion of
shame present in your body? If so, release it.

Can you imagine learning to relate to all enlightened expressions, either simultaneously or separately at different times during your life? Take the time to rest quietly and allow new life to gently find places in your heart and mind where it can begin to feel safe and at home. Be creative. Use your personal tools for finding peace. Allow your deep breathing to create new beginnings.

SECOND SPIRITUAL TOOL — BREATH OF LIFE

Throughout many years spent guiding people on sexual enlightenment journeys, I've encountered numerous reasons why people choose to explore and embrace the new paradigm of sexuality—to empower not just their physical bodies, but also their energy bodies. Some clients felt enticed by the spiritual nature of sexuality and wanted to learn more, while others were looking for alternatives to prescription drugs, which had side effects that inhibited sexual health. Some clients were teenagers seeking a better understanding of gender and sexuality, while others were parents, grandparents, and caretakers of small children and adolescents striving to protect, educate, and inspire their young charges with the truth about sexuality. But no matter how diverse their motivating factors, the Breath of Life technique became an essential part of their journey.

This powerful breathing technique has been assigned several names throughout the centuries. Its purpose, however, hasn't changed: use your breath and consciousness to energetically unite Earth and the cosmos as you become aware of and encourage the energy from both to flow through your energy core. Even if you are not aware of the divine gift, energy constantly circulates through your energy core as long as you are alive.

The healthy flow of energy within the body is vitally important for health on all levels. Deep and full breathing moves the energy that opens the door to your emotions, expands your personal consciousness, and ignites the transpersonal realm of Earth and the divine. Consciously using the Breath of Life technique to unite with this miraculous energy helps you relate well to your body's natural core and release any blocked energy in it. Breathing well is one of the best practices you can focus on to promote physical health, emotional well being, and mental brilliance. Breathing, like nature and sexual expression, is a powerful channel between the life of the senses and the divine. This spiritual tool must be learned before you can learn other powerful, spiritual tools for transporting and transmuting sexual energy presented later in this book.

Throughout the rest of your life, I strongly recommend that you use this three-step breathing technique to meditate daily for 15 minutes. Simply taking this daily energetic bath will help you make important changes in your life. Try it! Expect your life to change and savor the metamorphosis as it slowly or quickly happens in positive and meaningful ways.

⁂ STEP ONE: Position yourself so your back is straight and your shoulders are relaxed. Direct your mind to your pelvic floor and the warmth of Earth flowing into you. Close your mouth and inhale, pulling Earth's Divine Masculine and Divine Feminine energies up through your energy core all the way to the crown of your head and out to the cosmos. Visualize the energy instantly flowing up through your core from the bottom to the top. It will happen quickly with only a few breaths. Feel the slight tension and hear the sound of your breath in your nostrils, but not in your throat. Your inhale will be long and slow after you practice it. Relax your entire body, especially your belly, as you allow your lungs to receive precious oxygen.

ᨀ Step Two: While holding your breath, contract and expand the muscles twice that help you stop urinating. You have been practicing the contracting and expanding of these muscles all of your life so this step will be easy. With further practice, you will be able to isolate the pelvic floor and not use any other muscles. (Skip step two when teaching this technique to children.)

Exercising the pelvic floor muscles brings blood to the area. As a result, you may start to feel warmth or sexual energy in the genitals. Keeping the pelvic muscles healthy will help you have a better orgasm and strengthen your sexual energy! Furthermore, pumping the pelvic floor muscles while consciously breathing and visualizing helps transport sexual energy to the entire body. (The spiritual practice of drawing sexual energy out of the genitals and transporting it up into the belly, chest, throat, and brain is explained in Chapter 15.)

ᨀ Step Three: Direct your mind to the crown of your head and the divine masculine and feminine energies from the cosmos flowing into you. Open your mouth and exhale, guiding the energy down through your energy core all the way to the pelvic floor and into the Earth. Visualize the energy instantly flowing down through your core from the top to the bottom. Feel the slight tension and hear the sound of your breath in your throat, but not in your nostrils. The exhale will be long and slow after you practice it a few times. Relax your entire body, especially your belly and hips, as you allow your lungs to release precious carbon dioxide.

Repeat this three-step cycle over and over. As you do, you may start to release emotions. Simply allow them to flow while you continue your deep breathing. Learn to breathe slowly, fully, and deeply, paying attention to the fullness at the top of your inhale and the emptiness at the bottom of your exhale.

Inhaling and exhaling are metaphors for many universal truths. For example, your breath—the present moment—is all you have. It reminds you of the cycles of day and night, the waxing and waning of the moon, and the seasons of the sun. The inhale and exhale of breath represents birth, life, death, and rebirth.

When you practice Breath of Life meditation, you can become conscious of your union with Heaven and Earth in your energy essence—the inseparable Divine Masculine and Divine Feminine flow inside and around you. The divine union is the cosmos. Therefore, praying, breathing, and chanting are excellent vehicles for expressing appreciation and love before, during, and after this breathing meditation.

For Your Consideration: How did your body feel during the breathing exercise? Did you get dizzy? If so, you are breathing too quickly. Did inhaling seem easier or harder than exhaling? Practice making them equal in intensity and duration.

Practice acknowledging Earth and the cosmos united within and around you as a result of your conscious breathing and visualizing. Try breathing with a non-sexual partner. Look her or him directly in the eyes and notice the differences between breathing alone and breathing with a partner. This practice is great for people of any age. Have fun.

✦

Breathing or praying with your sexual partner is the first step toward learning how to be physically and sexually intimate while simultaneously relating to each other, your energy bodies, and the divine. Practice breathing together with eye contact. Create comfortable positions for facing each other so physical tension does not become a concern.

✦

When you are proficient at looking each other in the eyes while breathing, try breathing and holding each other without eye contact—focus instead on feeling the simultaneous contraction and expansion of your bodies.

✦

Do you and your partner feel comfortable praying or stating aloud your sacred intentions and appreciation for uniting your life force with the cosmos through breathing? The intimate communication with your partner and the divine may be one of the most intimate things you will ever do. It can take you to the center of what is most important in your lives together.

.⁓ 6 ⁓.

First Enlightened Expression—
Love the Human Body and the Earth

*T*he first enlightened expression of sexual energy is symbolized by the pelvic floor area of the body, specifically the anus. This enlightened expression is a reminder of how the powerful and creative life force that emanates from Earth influences our lives. Our healthy sexuality is directly related to our acceptance of the body and our personal reverence for its relationship with Earth—the human body is part of the body of Earth. Acknowledging this allows us to learn to accept and express our erotic, primal sexual energy because we are willing to honor and celebrate all of the body.

We are conscious of the fact that we learn about the sensuous and primal nature of our own bodies from the body of magnificent Earth. Long before our minds understand words, our bodies understand feelings. We learn about our senses from Earth. We hear, see, smell, taste, and touch Earth. We are not separate from Earth. We admit we are not only spiritual beings, but also physical beings. Therefore, we are willing to expand our awareness and consciousness of our thoughts and feelings about the human body.

Our relationship with Earth is our mirror for how we treat and feel about our bodies. We learn to feel awe, love, respect, and appreciation for Earth. Our hearts are filled with rapture because of its astounding power and beauty. We acknowledge Earth's never-ending gifts of life, and strive to not take them for granted or use them without appreciation. Then we learn to do the same for our bodies. We passionately feel the depth and fullness of the body's earthy nature through our erotic, sensuous, and fully open sexual expressions with our beloved partners.

One of the natural gifts of sexual energy is that we are responsible for our powerful sexual energy. All of our lives, we practice making choices about the use of sexual energy. We are not afraid of, nor do we deny, our powerful sexual energy. We practice loving the body and its relationship with Earth. However, if we think our bodies are imperfect, we do not avoid or repress the negative thinking. Rather, we address our difficult feelings—this sometimes requires professional help or counseling—in order to open up to love and intimacy. As a result, we learn to joyfully share our naked bodies and sexual energy with our partners.

Primal Sexual Energy

Primal sexual energy—lust—can be a very wonderful, positive, and highly charged force. Though this energy is impersonal, it can definitely be expressed in a personal way; in other words, with a beloved partner. A person who has never felt this intense, unbridled sexual desire is limited in the kinds of sexual expressions he or she is capable of experiencing. The profound pleasure and erotic intensity of the sexual desire for an intimate partner can be overwhelming. In this context, we learn to relate to, express, and enjoy the wild and tumultuous nature of Earth, which provides an astounding glimpse of the power of Earth's volcanic eruptions and earthquakes! This desire also helps us better understand the power of the divine. Embracing the body of a sacred partner and experiencing intense feelings of primal sexual energy are spiritually and sexually healthy occurrences that help us understand, in a small way, the power of eternal creation.

The excitement of lust can also be expressed in an impersonal way, with a person who is not necessarily known or cared about; in other words, through a casual sexual experience. Typically, both the person and the body are objectified in this type of experience. When impersonal primal sexual energy is combined with an impersonal expression, especially through sexually explicit pictures or videos—pornography—the experience can become problematic and eventually lead to danger or tragedy (see Chapter 9—Addiction). Moreover, sexual repression is equally ineffective and potentially dangerous and destructive. Thus, both sexual repression and sexual obsession can prevent sexual health and transformation.

How you use your primal sexual energy is up to you and directly related to how you use your primal life force, in general. You can choose to relate to sexual energy and its source, nature, and natural gifts. You can embrace and understand your primal power from Earth, and not be afraid of expressing it. Therefore, you can consciously express sexual energy in appropriate and empowering ways, especially by learning to change—transmute—primal sexual energy as described in Chapter 14.

For Your Consideration: How do you relate to and express your primal sexual energy? Are you balanced in its use or do you experience repression or obsession? Use your personal tools for expanding possibilities and finding clarity. Be courageous in your willingness to be honest.

✦

Now that you have read about the first enlightened expression of sexual energy, what is your relationship with destructive shame? If you believe shame is present in your body, take time now to release it. Monitor yourself carefully for the symptoms of shame as you read the rest of the chapter. Can you feel your relationship with the Divine Masculine and Divine Feminine within you?

THE RELATIONSHIP BETWEEN THE HUMAN BODY AND EARTH

Humans are increasingly learning that Earth is a living, purposive, and conscious nature and an organizing principle with its own ends, or natural gifts. Many believe Earth is a living organism, an intelligent being with a soul, striving to understand itself and evolve into a higher level of awareness. To help us understand and acknowledge the relationship between the human body and Earth, there are many interesting parallels and metaphors to consider. The following paragraph highlights only a few.

The circulation of water from the oceans to the clouds, lakes, creeks, and rivers and then back to the sea feeds and cleanses Earth. Likewise, our circulatory systems transport blood to feed and cleanse our bodies. About three-fourths of the mass of the human body is fluid and the same is true of Earth. The chemical makeup of blood resembles that of seawater. You can think of rivers that bring life to all as arteries and veins in the human body, and envision rain as the nurturing and fertilizing gift of the hormones, or sexual fluids. Just as the mighty rivers quietly meander or wildly rage, so can your sexual energy!

For Your Consideration: Have you ever been excited or overwhelmed when witnessing the power of Earth in the form of a wild river or raging ocean? Choose an appropriate time and place to imagine an aspect of Earth's power or beauty as being inside of you. Use your tools for transformation. Breathe fully and allow your senses to fill. As you feel awe in your heart, gently raise your sexual energy, but only as long as you can relate to Earth inside and around you. Remember the divine source of sexual energy. Record your feelings and thoughts.

What is your relationship with shame at this moment? Is it hiding in you or have you gratefully set it free? Are you breathing well? Are your sexual responses to the human body and Earth's nature based on your personal preferences of what is right for you in your life or are your choices based on other influences such as intimidation, fear, disgust, or shame?

※⊙※

Have you ever had the privilege of witnessing a wild animal quietly drink from a pool of life giving water? How does a cup of warm liquid feel as it slowly descends into and nourishes your body? Have you ever tasted life giving sexual fluids? Do you taste the tears or sweat of your lover? Have you tasted your urine? Why or why not?

※⊙※

Have you ever witnessed one of Earth's creatures give birth? Do you know how a woman's menstrual blood smells and tastes? Have you tasted the milk from a woman's breast? Why or why not? Could you pray or meditate at this moment, expressing your gratefulness for the Mystery of Life? Why or why not?

※⊙※

Being sexually intimate is a sacred celebration of life and death. Your body comes from Earth and it will return to Earth. Your beloved partner may die before you. If he or she does, you may deeply desire to see, taste, smell, hear, and feel him or her again—every single part! Do it now if it is possible. What are your responses to the above statement?

The breath of Earth—the gigantic respiratory system made of air, clouds, winds, and the atmosphere—is the breath of life for all. Humans also have a respiratory system that brings the breath of life to every cell in the body. Energy currents in the body are activated by breathing. When we are sexually expressive, we can allow the natural breath in Earth and us to flow as quietly as the doldrums in mid-ocean or as furiously as a tornado!

For Your Consideration: As you are well aware, Earth doesn't hold back! When it wants to be quiet, it is. When it wants to have a tornado fit, it does. Do you notice the breathing patterns of others who are not holding back such as children, athletes, and musicians?

Have you ever witnessed the first or last breath of one of Earth's beings?

Are you aware of your breathing patterns? Do you hold back or do you breathe freely? Are you aware of the different breathing sounds created while self-pleasuring or being intimate with your beloved? Listen carefully to your breath of life and love!

Can you express gratitude to your lover and your deity for
sacred breath? Can you do both while your sexual energy is
flowing? Why or why not?

༺✿༻

How are you breathing now? What is your relationship
with destructive shame at this moment? What is your rela-
tionship with the Divine Masculine and Divine Feminine
at this moment?

———————————————

Because metals, minerals, soil, and vegetation make up the
structure of land and mountains, we can think of them as Earth's
bones and skeleton. They are also the bones, skeleton, and muscles of the human body. You can get to know the human body
in the same way you might get to know your favorite mountain,
tree, or flower—by embracing every part, especially your genitals
and anus.

———————————————

For Your Consideration: Carefully look at your entire naked
body in the mirror—your hair, your eyes, your vagina or penis,
your fingernails, your anus. Do you have a favorite part of your
body? What about a least favorite part? How do you feel and
what do you think about your body? Are you breathing well?

༺✿༻

Take time to carefully touch all parts of your body. Breathe well. Send your entire body love and gratitude. Can you stand joyfully naked before your lover? Why or why not?

The sun, lightning, volcanoes, radiation, and electromagnetic fields create warmth and energy to sustain life on Earth. They also provide bodily heat, life energy, and the electromagnetic activity of the nervous system in the human body. We, too, can share our bodily heat, lightning and thunder, and volcanic eruptions with our sacred partners. Doing so deepens and strengthens the emotional, mental, sexual, and spiritual bonds between us.

For Your Consideration: Have you ever been riding a bike or motorcycle and noticed the air change temperatures as you passed through it? How about water temperatures while you were swimming in a lake, river, or ocean? Slowly try to experience the same thing with your body or your partner's body. Simply feel the varying temperatures of the body, depending on where and how you touch the miracle of life.

A SACRED PLACE

The oneness of Earth and the human body creates a magnificent place of belonging in the human psyche. As we grow and learn, we acknowledge that the land and the bodies in which we live are sacred. The idea of a sacred place is as old as life itself. For example, the South Rim of the Grand Canyon is a sacred place to the Havasupai Indians, who call it the Belly of the Mama.

There are many ways to acknowledge a sacred place. Our favorite gardens may become synonymous with sanctity. Sculptures and monuments in our environment may evoke a special sense of meaning. Buildings or structures can represent a place of meditation and learning, a background for dramatic presentations or ceremonies, a place for love and secrecy, or an expression of divine praise. Landscape paintings and photographs establish views of Earth that suggest a deep understanding of the land and our relationship with it, creating a sense of place that helps make geographical places an indelible part of our consciousness. Musical inspiration is deeply influenced by our sense of place. The times in which we live and cultural, environmental, rural, urban, and ethnic factors all combine to influence musical compositions in a way that makes them unique to us.

Telling personal stories is a way of acknowledging the power of a sacred place on Earth, a way of connecting with and sustaining it and the deeper meaning it represents. Generally, participants in sexual enlightenment workshops feel wonder, reverence, and tenderness when stories about sacred places and a oneness with Earth are shared. As they savor these moments, they discover the relationship between sacred places and healthy sexuality.

Once I left the town and country of my birth and started to travel as an adult, I lived with a sense that someday I would find a special place again that would awaken intensely deep emotions. I traveled the world, meeting the Mystery everywhere, but still longed to find something for which I had no words, no concepts—an unsettled desire for something critically important, yet forgotten. I listened to the call of the distant drum inside me, the nagging pressure of the invisible yearning that prevented me from being comfortable with my amnesic state.

In time, I would learn that the silent drumming was the constant call of Earth, my home, my ancestors, my body, asking to be consciously remembered and named. During retreats with Earth as part of my graduate studies, I would begin to name and articulate the forgotten parts:

> *After hiking several miles into the high and remote desert wilderness, I stop to rest. I realize I am entering a sacred place few people have entered; I am miles from dirt roads. I gaze upon the wild well of life—magnificent red sand, stately juniper and piñon pines, and ancient sagebrush. The recognition has finally started!*
>
> *"I have waited for so long to come here and be with all of you. I have waited for so long," I reverently whisper as my small hands quietly and slowly cover my body with hot red sand and feel its beloved recognition of me.*
>
> *I rest on the sandy, sacred altar. My voice is soft. Arms open. Heart full. I give thanks and weep as I speak, "Thank you for my home. I have so much love in my heart for you, my Lady. You are so beautiful. I have been waiting for so many years to come home. Such beauty, my Lady!"*

I kneel, arms and head prayerfully and reverently poised. My breathy sounds share my grateful thoughts, "I enter your divine well of life, your grand belly. I enter. I enter."

I crawl into our warm, sandy bed and lovingly whisper, "What is out there? What is out there, my Lady? Who are we?"

Eyes close. Sun blankets. Sleep awakens.

—An Excerpt from the Author's Academic Thesis

For Your Consideration: My experience with Earth in a sacred place is not unique. Do you have sacred places on Earth that you love? Have you given yourself the freedom to acknowledge and communicate your deep feelings with Earth? Use your tools for expanding consciousness and visit your sacred place in nature.

Is your body your sacred place? Do you strive to protect your physical body from the influences of negative thoughts, images, and trends in your community and the world that impersonalize, cheapen, and degrade your body? Use your tools for transformation and visit your personal sacred place—your body.

Are you aware of any of your own negative feelings and thoughts that would make you feel ashamed of your sacred, naked body? Can you choose to be joyfully naked and unashamed when you are sexual and intimate? Do you embrace all of your senses when you touch the body of an intimate partner in the same way you might embrace a sacred place in nature? If not, why?

How do you feel in your body at this moment? Are you breathing well? Remember, toxic shame will most likely stop your creative journey to sexual enlightenment if it is not recognized and released.

For various and important reasons, experiencing and honoring the common ground of all Earth's beings assists you in creating sexual enlightenment. When you identify with Earth's erotic beauty, you are able to carry its primal power and freedom into your sexual intimacy. Embracing a state of oneness with Earth helps you be humble, open-minded, and teachable because you are aware of a consciousness much bigger than your own—the divine gift of life energy available to everything in the cosmos. Therefore, the conscious experience of loving the physical body and filling the energy body with transmuted sexual energy— divine love and light—is obtainable.

PREGNANCY AND SACRED PLACES

A pregnant woman can become potently aware of her sacred place—her body becomes a vessel for receiving, creating, and sustaining new human life! Pregnancy and childbirth change a woman forever. Her consciousness is never the same, just as her body is never the same. She is not prepared for what she will experience once she becomes pregnant; her body does not just belong to her, but also to another human being. However, nine months of pregnancy may give her time to try and adjust to the primal energies taking charge of her life. Regardless of her positive or negative feelings about being pregnant, its reality is an enormous challenge, and she will need help and support from many directions.

After childbirth, her body, mind, and emotions need time—at least as long as she was pregnant—to adjust to the permanent changes in her life. A nursing mother takes even longer because her body is still sustaining the life of a new human being. Therefore, she probably will not regain a sense of autonomy until she stops nursing her baby. Some women never regain a sense of ownership of their sacred places, which can cause much tension in their lives and in their partners' lives.

If you are a new mother and feel bewildered, know that you are not alone. The tender stories of many new mothers are pulsing in the pages of this book. Regardless of the nature of your relationships with others—a new baby, other children, your partner, your friends, etc.—your most important relationship is with your own body. Therefore, after pregnancy, it is critical that you reclaim your body as your most important relationship and place in the world.

Arguably, at no other time in your life will your relationship with Earth be more healing. You will need time to find and claim your Earth body within—your clear rivers, towering mountains, hot deserts, and quiet breezes. When the time is right, Earth will once again reintroduce you to erotic sexual passion. If allowed, compassionate Earth will call upon and unite you with the consciousness of your ancient ancestors—women throughout time who have given birth to other human beings.

Women are reverently and eternally united in their creative, dangerous journeys because they instinctively discover during childbirth that birth and death are lovers.

POWER SPOTS

On Earth there are special places of power. They are called power spots. We feel drawn or guided to these power spots by a source beyond our normal awareness or consciousness. When we surrender to their magnetic calls and travel to their origins, we become emotionally aroused upon arriving at our destination. Then something triggers and shifts our mindset into a new dimension of consciousness, and unusual events take place in which our normal frame of reference is nonexistent. These personal experiences with Earth are intense and engage our minds, bodies, and spirits. An extraordinary feeling of unity with reality occurs. When our expanded state of consciousness returns to normal, we experience personal and meaningful changes in our lives.[1]

It's as if these points on the Earth's body are calling to us over and over again. A person who has had a spiritual experience at a powerful place understands the meaning and value of power spots. Lourdes, Machu Picchu, the Ganges River, Mount McKinley, Mount Sinai, Mecca, Mount Kilimanjaro, Delphi, Jerusalem, Mount Everest, Mount Fuji, Glacier National Park, the Grand Canyon, the Amazon River, Victoria Falls, and the Sahara Desert are just a few of Earth's power spots.

The human body also has power spots. We can acknowledge and become intimate with our personal erogenous power spots.

When we explore and claim them, we learn to acknowledge direct experiences with our life force. It is important that we learn to claim our personal power and that we practice making choices about its appropriate use. We also must practice remembering the source of our sexual energy—it's an inheritance from the divine. Then when we feel the primal, erotic energy of Earth in us, we'll remember that we are grand spiritual beings whose essence runs through and around our physical bodies. We'll also be able to claim the divine guiding power that runs through our essence and the Earth's primal power that runs through our physical bodies.

It's important to recognize that Earth's astounding primal power and beauty create mystical states in us. These heightened, spiritual conditions always take place after we have been in contact with something regarded as beautiful, valuable, or both. Therefore, Earth's beauty creates mystical states that open us to receiving guidance and inspiration from the divine. Just as Earth's beauty and wildness lead us home to our spiritual centers, so does our bodies' beauty and wildness! Thus, we can learn to be comfortable with intense primal energy during sexual experiences because we understand the spiritual relationship of Earth and God.

Conscious Touch, a wonderful tool for exploring touch, is described in detail in Chapter 12. This technique allows us to safely discover and explore our sacred places and power spots, and to embrace what we may have alienated from our consciousness. Be aware that the extent to which we are alienated from Earth is the extent to which we are alienated from our bodies and, unfortunately, human alienation from Earth is a more dangerous, severe, and chronic state than most people realize.

Notes: Chapter 6—First Enlightened Expression—Love the Human Body and the Earth

[1]Swan, *Sacred Places: How the Living Earth Seeks Our Friendship,* 1990.

◈ 7 ◈

SECOND ENLIGHTENED EXPRESSION —
HONOR GENDER

*T*he second enlightened expression of sexual energy is symbolized by the area of the genitals, both inside and outside the body. When we are young, it soon becomes obvious that this part of the body teaches us about the pleasant life force that flows throughout the whole body. As divine energy passes through the genitals, it is felt as sexual energy more than in any other place in the body! Denying the feeling is difficult—it can feel wonderfully intense! We learn to understand and accept the divine source and nature of our sexual energy so as we grow and mature, we can explore the natural gifts of sexual energy in healthy and joyful experiences.

One of the nine natural gifts of sexual energy is that it helps us better understand and relate to gender. No other area of the body reveals such physical differences between men and women as the genitals. Perhaps to most people, gender appears to be a simple and obvious fact of life: there are men and there are women, and the physical differences are obvious. On the other hand, there are differences that can be mysterious and confusing. Sometimes, the differences are painfully apparent. Other times, the differences are joyfully apparent. As we all know, relationships between men and women can be awesome, but they can also be awful.

Most people do not take time to seriously and honestly explore the issues surrounding the differences between men and women. Yes, in varying degrees, we strive to explore the political and economical differences, and we must. But how many people sincerely ask these questions: "In the deepest and fullest sense, what does it mean to be a woman? What does it mean to be a man?" So much can be learned by genuinely asking the questions. How many people fully appreciate and love being a gendered human being? How many people sincerely honor and respect the opposite sex? As we successfully ask questions and open up to receive answers, we become conscious of what it really means to be a sexual man or woman.

WHAT DOES IT MEAN TO BE A MAN?

While a man may feel relatively successful and sexually fulfilled—he is satisfied with the strength of his erections and orgasms and confident in his ability to initiate and guide touch, be sexually intimate, and give his partner great pleasure—he may not be fully conscious of what it means to be a man. Therefore, his sexual expression is no more than adequate![1]

Why? Because when a man gives and receives pleasure with his partner, he also reveals the unconscious understanding and experiences of his gender. Perhaps, he is too busy trying to be a good man and partner to take the time to know himself better, to learn to honestly love and honor the man he is. He may not be aware of his life's purpose. He may be continually working hard to provide for, protect, and instruct those for whom he feels love and responsibility. Taking the time to deeply wonder what it really means to be a man is something he hasn't done.

A man who clearly understands and respects the great gifts of his masculinity is a man who honors his gender. Ideally, he is aware of and appreciates his natural ability to create in the world with confidence, to bravely focus and direct his will against great obstacles, and to have faith in life and his part in the miracle. He honors his gifts of leadership and protection. As he allows his holy inner knowing to lead him into his life's purpose, he gives the fruits of his great and courageous labor to his partner, his family, and humanity, joining the ranks of honorable men throughout all time. He loves and receives himself with great compassion. He gratefully receives his unique, divine essence. And finally, when he brings the consciousness and strength of his sexual focus to his partner, he is a wild, protective, loving, sensitive sexual warrior because he knows what it means to be a man. Throughout his life, he will continue to explore and honor the masculine gift of life that he has been given.

Moreover, an honorable man has an inner sense of worth, responsibility, and self-love because it is directly related to his spirituality. If a man understands his inner masculine and feminine energies, he can relate them to the perfect flow of the Divine Masculine and the Divine Feminine—and infinitely expand his consciousness. As a man grows and matures, this understanding prepares him for a healthy life and relationship.

Additionally, if a man accurately understands how much his feminine partner cherishes his manhood, he will want to carry the depth of his understanding and consciousness into his friendship and relationship with her. When a man who has developed this consciousness reaches out to his sacred lover and leads her into sexual intimacy and love, he intentionally and consciously brings her his direct lineage to all honorable men. In other words, he brings God to her. Consequently, she is never the same! He knows how to simultaneously feel his life force and his oneness with God. He leads her into the experience of transmuting sexual energy to transform their love and lives.

For Your Consideration: Do you have a sense of the natural configuration of your core energies? Are the energies healthy?

If you are male, what does it mean to you to be a man? Have you taken time to discover your life's purpose? Do you honor and appreciate your masculine qualities? In your unique ways, how do you express your masculinity? Who are your mentors and heroes? Would you include yourself among the honorable men of all time? Do your family and friends honor you?

If you don't love yourself, what must you do to grow and change? Would it involve having a different relationship with the divine? How can you relate to your masculine essence and sexual energy in order to grow and evolve? Subsequent chapters will provide insights to these questions to help you as you continue on your journey.

✦

What is your relationship with destructive shame? What is your relationship with Earth? What is your relationship with your spirituality?

✦

If you are a woman, ask yourself these same questions in relation to your inner masculine and the Divine Masculine.

Being a woman, I obviously do not know what it means to be a man. However, I do know what it means to visit with thousands of men in my office, to listen to them share their successes and failures, and to watch them relate to me from their fascinating masculine essences. I have witnessed them revealing their strength and amazing focus; striving to be better lovers, partners, or husbands; willing to share their deepest sorrows and confusion; and always wanting—sometimes desperately—to understand their lovers.

I adore honorable men. To me, they are absolutely astounding, and I feel privileged to be in their presence. The world is blessed to have men who live from a place of strength, caring, and courage, to have men who are willing to get up every day, slay their inner demons and dragons, and go forth in faith toward their inspired goals and life's natural gifts. Typically, they are willing to give everything they have—courage, focused mind and purpose, honorable use of power in the world, protection, guidance, money, and sexual passion—to their partners. They are willing to give all that they have because they quietly, yet naturally, want to be received and adored. My prayer is that the world will wildly love them.

Honorable men are my heroes. One of the most amazing men I have ever known and loved is also my favorite hero—my father, who died this year in the presence of his four loving daughters and the silent, spirit essence of his eternal wife of 65 years who died three months earlier.

What Does It Mean to Be a Woman?

While a woman may feel relatively successful and sexually fulfilled—she gladly opens her body to her sacred partner, feels confident and satisfied with giving and receiving pleasure, and feels at ease in her orgasmic body—she may not be fully conscious of what it means to be a woman. Therefore, her sexual expression is no more than adequate!

Why? Because when a woman gives and receives pleasure with her adored partner, she also reveals the unconscious understanding and experiences of her gender. Perhaps, she is too busy trying to be a good woman and partner to take the time to know herself better, to learn to honestly love and honor the woman she is. She may be continually working hard to receive, care for, and nurture those for whom she feels love and responsibility. She, like many women, has not taken the time to seriously and honestly explore what it means to be a woman beyond the obvious.

A woman who takes the spiritual and emotional journey into her femininity longs to understand and feel who she is in her fullness and to communicate this passion with her beloved partner. She willingly partakes of and expresses the breathtaking gift of her inner and outer beauty. She prays for and meditates on the ability to open up to and live in the fullness of her mysterious feminine heart of love and the truth of her emotions. In her warm and earthy body, she tenderly, wildly, and sensuously opens her heart, mouth, arms, and legs to receive her lover. She is the call of her own feminine fullness. She opens up to and receives her own sweet, gentle exquisiteness. A woman who lives this reality in her sexual loving opens up all that is possible to her sacred lover. She is able to do this because she knows what it means to be a woman and feels safe being one.

Most importantly, she consciously offers her lover an inner awareness of the Divine Feminine who has waited for eons with warmth and patience as women learn and claim what it means to be a feminine woman. A woman's "wombheart" feels her Divine Feminine. Therefore, because she is safe and protected, she flies into the wildness of Earth that cannot be contained and offers her lover the gift that is her body's spiritual birthright. She consciously opens the door to the rapture of cosmic freedom into which her partner longs to release. This wondrous miracle she momentarily offers to her partner transforms him forever because she consciously brings her Goddess to him. A woman may strive her entire life to create the consciousness to offer such a gift from her feminine essence.

For Your Consideration: Do you have a sense of the natural configuration of your core energies? Are the energies healthy and flowing well?

If you are female, have you taken the time to consider what it really means to be a woman? Who are you? Are you trying to discover and live from the inner and outer beauty of your feminine essence?

✿

Do you know how to return to your feminine essence at the end of a long day in which you used your inner masculine to teach and care for children or to work and compete in the world? Do you understand how critical it is to the world for women to live from their feminine essences? Who are your feminine role models?

✿

Would you say that you are an emotionally open and loving woman? Are you protected and guided by men, friends, and family so you can remain open and loving?

✿

If you hide your feminine essence or do not love it, what could you do to change how you feel? How can you relate to the Divine Masculine and Divine Feminine to grow and evolve?

✿

What is your relationship with toxic shame? What is your relationship with Earth? What is your relationship with the Divine Feminine? What is your relationship with the Divine Masculine?

If you are a man, ask yourself these same questions in relation to your inner feminine and the Divine Feminine.

It is my prayer that all my sisters will discover and live from their exquisite, Divine Feminine essence. The journey may be intense and will most likely require a vigilant commitment to addressing and releasing the illusion of destructive shame, just as it has for many women who have learned about sexual enlightenment in workshops and private sessions. Share your story with others, as I am willing to share my story with you.

Through the wilderness retreats and my spiritual relationship with Earth's nature, I begin to heal my vague, constant sense of incompleteness. The healing spontaneously begins simply because I am communing with Earth—my body, my lover, my healer, my friend. I feel the Divine Feminine, my Lady, through my love for Earth.

As the winding, dry creek bed leads me into the high desert wilderness, I walk quickly, being careful not to hurt or threaten those who inspire me, those whose home I temporarily invade. The hot, quiet breeze surrounds me, caresses me, shields me from thoughts, and allows me to feel cool sweat as it tastes my skin. I hear the buzzing of a determined fly that momentarily bumps into me, and then hurries on its way. I smile and wonder where it is going so quickly.

I rest.

In silence, I pray, "Oh yes, my Lady, open me! Teach me who I am." Earthlings notice as I share my thoughts and shed my shield. Labor begins. Intimacy and vulnerability are born.

Gratefully naked, I stand legs apart, feet holding firmly, arms raised and praising, Sun kissing and washing me down. Wisely and knowingly, Wind leads me to the door of my inner home, the place where truth resides. I feel my Lady's thoughts— She who enters my heart and speaks through my love.

Slowly, my hands cover my belly. I allow my pride, shame, and confusion to sink into warmth and safety. Muscles relax. Womb opens. I rub my belly, an area in my body where I have caged the dark soul of shame. I prepare to become one with Earth, whose wisdom opens my cage door.

Earth is hot. I am sweat. We melt. Earth is my lover. Earth is my body.

I kneel. Slowly and carefully my small hands push the sand aside as I prepare to be received, to be held. Spreading my arms and feet, breathing deeply, feeling safe, feeling wanted, feeling loved, I meet my lover.

Silently, my Lady tells me to release the dark confusion in my sweet belly into the shallow altar of sand. Psychically, I see and feel the thick, black energy drain into Earth as She tenderly holds me like a small frightened bird, allowing me to feel warm and safe, preparing me to fly.

Carefully, silently I breathe. Barely audible, I speak Her words as I feel them caressing me, "My child, I prepare you. My child, I purify you. Let me hold you, beautiful one. Let it drain from your belly. You and all my daughters have carried old wounds too long. Let Sun purify you."

Accompanied by gentle rocking and sobbing, I offer sounds of praise, "Mother, my Lady." Chanting leads me further into Her until softly, and then in silence, I wait.

"Stand tall. Stand strong. Know who you are, my beautiful one" She silently directs. Feet wide and arms stretched, I chant in a strong voice.

I am finished. I am empty. I am full.

I breathe deeply once and immediately feel the need to turn quickly and fly away, to feel my body open to my surroundings and receive Sun. Firm strides carry me and my wide smiles for miles without stopping, lifting us down and off the mountain toward the familiar draw and the ancient boulders' memories of times past.

—An Excerpt from the Author's Academic Thesis

My conscious decision to explore the meaning of sexual health and enlightenment by learning to honor my feminine gender began when I learned to relate to Earth as my confidant and healer. The freedom, adoration, and ecstatic states I felt with Earth set the course—my feminine tenderness and vulnerability were nurtured and witnessed.

My experiences are not necessarily ones to emulate. Rather, they are simply examples of one person's path. I share my stories with the hope that they will help you to set your own course, to personalize and articulate your own needs and desires as a gendered human being.

A willingness to awaken to and honor the truth of gender is central to creating a worldwide sexual evolution—a spiritual state free of destructive shame and ignorance. The power of our sexuality is more than we ever imagined when we, as intimate, committed lovers, offer our gifts of honored gender to each other. In our intimate, sexual, and loving togetherness, we begin to feel within and between us what it means to be the Divine Feminine and the Divine Masculine. We can spend our entire lives preparing to create this expanded state of consciousness. Furthermore, to expand our consciousness, we would identify and explore helpful personal traits and qualities. For example, we would strive to be present and conscious in the moment; we would deepen our faith in the goodness and possibilities of life; and we would believe in ecstasy.

Notes: Chapter 7 — Second Enlightened Expression — Honor Gender

[1]Deida, *Finding God Through Sex*, 2004.

~ᴓ 8 ᴓ~

Third Enlightened Expression —
Embrace Masculine
Sexual Energy

*T*he third enlightened expression of sexual energy is symbolized by the solar plexus, the area just below the rib cage. This part of the body is not entirely encased by the rib cage or the hips so it is vulnerable and in need of protection. Since masculine energy offers protection, it is easy to remember that the third enlightened expression is about healthy masculine sexual expression in men and women. Masculine energy helps us be focused, goal oriented, perceptive, and initiatory in our sexuality. It takes us out into the world of possibilities with confidence so we can face obstacles and achieve goals.

Typically more prevalent in males, masculine energy enables a man to initiate touch with confidence so he can lead his partner into sexual expression and orchestrate and guide their interactions. His inner masculine enables the flow—the cycle of initiating, opening, releasing, and receiving—of masculine and feminine energies to begin between them. The masculine energy in him initiates and penetrates physically by entering the body of his lover. It initiates and penetrates emotionally by entering her heart. And it initiates and penetrates spiritually by pervading her body with consciousness.

Masculine energy wants to be emptied by sex; freedom fulfills the masculine sexual essence. Its goal is to engage in sexual activity and allow energy to flow. It travels into the lover and determines the depth of sexual experience.[1] Therefore, when a man initiates touch, he wants his partner to be interested in opening to him. He releases his energy and conscious mind and body into his beloved partner because he wants to be received. Sex happens in his genitals. His pleasure comes from knowing his partner is pleased. By giving, he is received. He will relate to his feminine partner because his goal is to feel sexual energy and release into her. Conversely, she feels sexual energy and receives him because she wants to relate to him. The differences between their motives are quite profound.

To understand these differences, we must first remember that sexual energy is a neutral life force. We can choose to express this energy in conscious or unconscious ways, in sacred or profane experiences. It is our choice. When we are educated about the nature, source, and natural gifts of sexual energy, we have the freedom to make more choices about how we express this life force. The next step in understanding the profound differences between the sexual needs of masculine men and feminine women is to remember that the masculine sexual energy in men (and women) naturally leads to impersonal expressions of sexual energy. Because men, in general, carry significantly more masculine energy than women, it is easier for a masculine man to have an impersonal sexual experience than it is for a feminine woman. Masculine energy allows men and women to set and meet goals while feminine energy allows them to feel and know if the goals are appropriate.

Consequently, it is critical that we remember the following: the feminine is protected by the masculine. It is only through feminine energy that we recognize whether our sexual goals are appropriate, safe, and healthy; feel our emotions; and know if we are in love with our lives. Spiritually and sexually, the quiet, inner voice helps us to know and feel what is appropriate. When the feminine center, the chest, swells with loving energy, we feel whole and balanced. Then, we are able to learn the truth and consequences of sexual expression.

A feminine woman does not sexually initiate as naturally as a masculine man. However, it is something she can certainly learn to do. She learns by watching her partner use his masculine energy when they are passionate and erotic. She understands the flow of masculine and feminine energies within her and between them, and she feels safe and protected. Consequently, she learns the great pleasure of initiating, directing, and leading her intimate partner in their sexual expressions. Because she understands the flow of the masculine and feminine energies within her body, she knows it is a perfectly healthy flow. It is a wise woman who knows that most men would love to have their sacred lovers initiate sexually! They would love to be seduced.

In a sexually expressive man, the inner strength of healthy masculine and feminine energies provides the understanding and honoring of boundaries and communication. One of the natural gifts of sexual energy is that it teaches us how to use our sexual energy, and therefore, energy in general. An honorable, masculine man has no interest in taking advantage of or having power over his partner. He guides and directs with awareness and sensitivity because his inner flow of masculine and feminine energies is awake and conscious. He understands that the purpose of masculine energy in both men and women is to protect the feminine in men and women, to protect the world and Earth.

For Your Consideration: The masculine qualities of determination and courage enliven the mind and spirit. They move visions and great insights into action — the determining gift of human purpose. Do you have masculine heroes? Why or why not?

The confidence and drive of masculine energy in men and women have created astonishing changes in the last century. A healthy flow of masculine and feminine energies within and between people, especially in relation to governments, corporations, and countries, is critical during such intense periods of change. Without the energetic flow of masculine and feminine energies, human beings do not recognize whether or not their goals are healthy, honorable ones that benefit all of Earth's beings. At no other time on Earth has the healthy flow of masculine and feminine energies been more critical than the present. The following story illustrates this point.

Not wanting to be late, I hurried out the trailer door, fumbling as I searched in the dark for my bike—the only means of rapid transportation available to me at my home on the three-mile-long island far out in the vast reaches of the Pacific Ocean. Though feeling somewhat tense and nervous, I was able to enjoy the softly sparkling Christmas lights as I pedaled my rusty bike the one block that separated me from the end of the island. As I sat down on the lap of the warm beach, my friend, Wind, teasingly tried to coax me into abandoning all reason and care from my anxious mind.

The tide, visiting elsewhere on Earth, had temporarily rolled away, exposing the gurgling sounds and mysterious creatures of the coral reef that connected the family of tiny islands of the Kwajalein Atoll. Perhaps sensing the need to protect, light clouds were trying to gather around our little corner of the Marshall Islands.

In the dark distance, I could hear the familiar, soothing brum-brum-brum of a small motorboat slowly carrying Marshallese workers back to their tin-shack homes on Ebeye, a mile-long ghetto island, after their day's work. I thought of these people, as I often did, and remembered how they had traded their ancient friendship and passion for Mother Sea for televisions, canned vegetables, and U.S. government subsidies. I remembered that some of them had faithfully, but naively, believed the U.S. military officials who promised them not only money, but also the freedom to return to their home, Bikini Island, as soon as the nuclear bomb tests were completed. Not wanting to cage the soul of painful feelings, I breathed, and in doing so, opened myself to the waiting memories of the beautiful singing voices of the Ebeye children who were my students. As always, my heart ached with love for them, for their courage, kindness, and gentleness in the face of poverty, disease, and hopelessness. Wanting to stay visually alert, I asked Wind to breathe through me as I refocused my attention and looked toward Sky.

I felt blessed because I knew few people had ever seen what I was about to witness. As I sat impatiently, my ears responding to the demanding calls of the reef creatures, a bright light appeared suddenly in Sky as though responding to my demanding thoughts. I was able to finally see it, the bright star from the East! I gasped for breath as the fiery object shot toward me in its bright, beautiful glory! Never had I seen such fireworks! Closer and closer it blazed, until suddenly it split into several parts, each flying toward me, creating a new design, a brilliant tripod-path in Sky! Instinctively, I fell to the sand and covered my head.

As quickly as it had appeared, the fiery display disappeared. Sky was in shock. Not even silence spoke.

I, too, sat speechless, not able to breathe or move. I joined and sought safety in the void, the spacelessness at the bottom of my exhale. I was buried in the moment, wanting to be reborn. I strained to focus, to think clearly about what had just taken place. I struggled for words that would separate me from the totality of my experience, for words to define it and, therefore, me. Then, I began to breathe.

I also began to remember. What I had witnessed was created with the genius of the human mind. I had witnessed the incredibly breathtaking display of colors a person would see seconds before she or he was annihilated, perhaps seconds before the human race was annihilated. I struggled for more words.

What was its name? Oh yes, it was called MX ICBM. What does the acronym mean? I remembered the words—multiple warhead intercontinental ballistic missile. The ideas were coming more quickly now, and my physical feelings were less-ening in intensity as I focused my consciousness on each new concept and definition. I had witnessed technology invented through the incredibly creative yet horribly destructive capacity of the human mind.

The missile I had just watched enter the lagoon was designed and programmed to shoot into the atmosphere, out into space, and then reenter the atmosphere. It was launched from Vanden-berg Air Force Base in California, and was being tracked con-stantly by scientists at Kwajalein Island Missile Range. At some predetermined altitude, each independently targeted, unarmed warhead searched for its individual target and landed within a few feet of its desired location. In twenty minutes, they had trav-eled 10,000 miles. Simultaneously, fear and awe short-circuited my brain; again, I became numb.

As I stumbled back up the beach and headed toward home, I began to hear the sounds of music, each tone aimed at and searching for my brainhaze, calling me, helping me, loving me. I recognized the sounds and words of Christmas carolers singing, "Peace on Earth, good will toward men."

I thought of some of the men I had known and loved. I sent them thoughts of peace and good will: the behavioral psy-chologist, the mechanical engineer, the medical doctor, the gla-ciologist, the jet pilot. These kind and brilliant men were trained to use their minds in the same ways as those who created the missile.

By separating, dissecting, and defining, all of them dis-ciplined their consciousness to focus primarily on logic and discrimination. To them, the application of scientific principles was most likely the best and most reliable way to prove, dis-prove, or define "reality." But to me, reality was personal. It could not necessarily be proven, though aspects could be shared. I believed the application of scientific principles could be effective, but that it was only one of the many ways to search for knowledge. Definitions could block as well as open communication.

Being aware of my thoughts about men and science, I felt the movement of my bike as the wheels slowly rolled along the coral road and swayed with the rhythm of my body. Choosing to get closer to Mother, I jumped off my bike, took off my shoes, and felt her warm support. Then I slowly lifted my head to greet the penetrating smell of my friend, Rain. I stood in my small front yard, listened to the palm fronds fiddle in the breeze, and received the moist sweetness of various tropical blossoms. As I opened the door to my little trailer and embraced my warm husband, I heard the faint, final words of the carolers' lullaby as the sounds faded like gentle snow over the calm village, magically sighing, whispering to everything, everywhere:

"Sleep in heavenly peace."

"Heavenly peace."

"Peace."

"Peace."

I prayed for the same.

—An Excerpt from the Author's Journal

The above story illustrates the need for balance between masculine and feminine energies. The appropriateness of the creative and destructive capacity of masculine energy—focused and projected mind-missiles—can only be known when it releases into and is cradles by the feminine womb of love and appreciation. To put it another way, thoughts (masculine energy) and feelings (feminine energy) are both necessary to accurately determine the worthiness of goals. The safety, peace, and prosperity of the world depend on the health and natural relationship of masculine and feminine energies within and between people. Healthy sexual intercourse and expression are metaphors for the inner strength of the healthy masculine and feminine energies of men and women around the world who exemplify an understanding and honoring of boundaries and communication.

For Your Consideration: Masculine energy enables us to meet challenges and solve problems. What do you think about your ability to solve problems and create changes in your life based on goals you feel are healthy?

The above question may be especially painful for men to answer. If it is painful for you, courageously wrap your heart around shame—the Great Illusion—and set it free. If you are proud of your ability to create movement in your life, celebrate joyfully. It is a wonderful strength!

When men and women learn to use the power of masculine energy within and between people to obtain great goals, the results can be astounding for the world. The flow of masculine and feminine energies is healthy when it is complete and unbroken. However, weak feminine energy that won't draw the masculine to it leaves the world unconscious. Conversely, unbridled masculine energy that won't enter the feminine leaves the world dangerously unprotected. Thus, we must understand what causes the energy flow to break.

How the Energy Cycle Stops

One defining aspect of being human is that we are limited in certain perceptions and abilities, which depend on various factors, many of which are out of our control. Therefore, we may only see a small part of the entire picture of life. Another defining aspect of being human is that we constantly relate to the energies in our energy core—we are constantly adjusting and readjusting the flow of masculine and feminine energies within us and between us and other people. Consequently, we spend our entire lives learning and growing from our choices. The ideal state—what we are striving to obtain—is a healthy flow of masculine and feminine energies in our unique energy centers. Furthermore, a spiritual relationship with the cosmos—the Divine Feminine and Divine Masculine energies within the energy core—creates an expanded state of consciousness that miraculously amplifies our ordinary perceptions and abilities. Such is our tender, unique nature.

However, if we pollute our inner temples—our energetic essences and divine homes—we cannot open up to and receive the peace, love, and guidance we desire and need for successful experiences on Earth. We cannot expect to be healthy when we fail to keep our inner rivers pure and free from worldly influences. We weaken our natural relationship with divinity when we allow anything in our lives to become more important. It doesn't matter if it is our partners, children, families, religious structures, friends, emotions, work, homes, animals, money, sex, food, freedom, power, beauty, ideas, philosophies, health, drugs, alcohol, communities, etc. When we place too much importance on these things, we distort the influence of the perfect love and protection of the Divine Masculine and Divine Feminine within us.

Consequently, the flow of masculine and feminine energies within and between us and others also becomes distorted. It becomes weakened. It breaks down. Thus, we have difficulty relating well to the ups and downs of life. For example, we may experience confusion, tension, heartache, health issues, financial concerns, loneliness, sexual issues, legal problems, spiritual and psychic angst, and so forth. And when we suffer, our relationships suffer.

If our partners are unaware of the nature, source, and natural gifts of sexual energy, if we are unaware of the masculine and feminine energies within and between us, if we forget that the divine loves and guides us, or if we pollute our inner sacred homes, our relationships are in trouble. The masculine may not initiate, the feminine may not open, the masculine may not release, or the feminine may not receive. The sacred relationship is weakened and it may break. This principle is true, regardless of sexual orientation; it is based on energy, not gender.

WHEN THE MASCULINE STOPS THE FLOW OF ENERGIES

The flow of the energy cycle stops when the masculine in men and women will not initiate an energetic relationship with the feminine or when the masculine will not release into the feminine.

This creates tension in and between people and breeds sexual disinterest and dysfunction between partners—pressing personal concerns are one of the most common reasons why men and women seek illumination and sexual health. Those who have been successful in their quests for sexual enlightenment were committed and patient. They achieved their goals because they were humble, openminded, and teachable. They were willing to embrace and honor the common ground of all beings, and to acknowledge fear, release it, and open up to love. By developing a wise understanding of the flow of masculine and feminine energies, they learned to recognize when and how it becomes blocked, empowering themselves to reestablish a healthy flow.

In Him: A man may not initiate with his partner or with his inner feminine for many reasons. He may have lost confidence in himself. His masculine energy may have become unfocused, weak, timid, or wounded, or it may have lost its power and strength. He may have lost track of his life's purpose or intense responsibilities may have distracted him from his primary relationship with his partner. The masculine man may be concerned that he will be lost or consumed by the intense emotions of the feminine.

Sometimes, a man may have such difficulty addressing his deep inner turmoil—blocked feminine energy caused by the inability and unwillingness of the masculine to engage the feminine trauma—that he becomes emotionally ill. Post-traumatic stress disorder is an example of what happens when the energetic relationship of the masculine and feminine fails to flow properly. Violence in all forms can create the dysfunction of a traumatized feminine or unwilling masculine.

I was once married to a brilliant, handsome, and intensely masculine man who became emotionally distant and sexually withdrawn because, tragically, he could not flow energetically into his horrified, inner feminine world.

Too often I hear the garbled shouting and crying of his dreamtime conversations as he wrestles and pleads with haunting, horrible Warwound. The noble, wounded warrior's dreamtime and daytime are not companions and do not relate, nor can they name or define each other. During daytime, he is a focused, confident, and highly skilled pilot. During dreamtime, he is the courageous, wild pilot and squadron leader who flies through the screams and moans of his horrified self, helping and directing soldiers at war to fight and kill. The two men never meet. Consequently, the flow of his life pulse has been put on automatic pilot. The lack of reconciliation between his disparate parts drains, cripples, and oppresses his kind and sensitive self.

As a child and young male, the patriotic citizen was taught that it was his duty as a man to go to war and protect his family and country. He still deeply loves his country. He still believes in protecting others, though he no longer can because he is broken. He knows he can't bring himself or me wholeness; his anger conceals the truth. But, his silence speaks loudly to me, "You go on, Kristin. You go on alone. I am tired now. Let me rest. You explore for both of us. Find what I have lost. Find feelings that I cannot access, inner meanings that I cannot even imagine exist."

And so I must.

—An Excerpt from the Author's Journal

There are other reasons why the masculine may no longer initiate or release into the feminine. For various reasons, a man may no longer be drawn to his partner. He may not be attracted to her physical or inner beauty. Her emotions may detract or confuse him. He may not find her loving and kind. He may find she lacks vibrancy in her body, in her willingness to embrace the beauty of life. He may not believe in her.

Men can objectify women. When this happens, men are not in contact with their inner feminine. They may be addicted, in a sense, to their own masculine energy. In this case, they would be driven—constantly on the go and continually working—but unable to find inner peace. They would be attracted to women primarily as sexual vehicles. Thus, they might be harsh, shrill, and shallow in their feelings and thoughts. In working with men struggling with these types of concerns, the key driver in their quest for sexual enlightenment was their desire to take charge of their out of control lives. Often, as they shared their stories, they acknowledged deep shame and regret.

For Your Consideration: Healthy masculine energy is critical for a masculine man. If you are male, how healthy is your masculine essence? If it is weak, wounded, or disinterested in feminine energy, either sexually or otherwise, great care must be taken to promote healing. To love and honor your power in the world, clarify your relationship with the Divine Masculine and Divine Feminine.

Are your sexual goals honorable? Use your tools for transformation to deeply explore this question.

At this moment, what is your relationship with destructive shame? What is your relationship with the Divine Masculine and Divine Feminine?

IN HER: When a woman's partner will no longer bring himself to her, it can be very difficult. The experience can cause a feminine woman serious emotional turmoil, especially if her own inner masculine is undeveloped or wounded. Her heart may ache, and her mind may become confused. Without her inner masculine or partner to help move and guide her through her pain, she may turn to something other than her divine center to fill her.

She may turn to food, books, children, religion, family, service work, her career, etc., hoping they will dull the pain so she can feel a sense of fullness, of happiness. And though these things may interest her and help, they may never replace the expression of love and fullness she felt in relation to her partner. She may come to believe she is no longer a desirable woman. Therefore, she may lose the ability to feel and believe in her beauty, love, and passion. Because her own natural masculine is weak or wounded, she may enter into emotional doldrums. This deep longing can be destructive and dangerous.

When this happens, she is lost. She will have to work hard to find her flow again. If she is not conscious of her thoughts and feelings, creating a flow of life energies that brings joy and peace may be very difficult. There is nothing more painful for a woman than admitting she doesn't feel beautiful or lovable. Her belief in her ugliness is spiritual pollution. It is like being buried alive, but being too numb to know. This fear and toxic shame may consume her. Her masculine energy is not strong enough to push her out of her feminine emotional cage. The flow has stopped.

The individual stories of this group of women are painful both to share and to hear. Fortunately, there is an awakening and healing process that begins when they understand and begin to feel the sacred, energetic flow of divine power and love.

For Your Consideration: Healthy masculine energy is critical for a woman. If her masculine is weak or wounded, or if her feminine essence is unwilling to open up to or receive the masculine, great care must be taken to promote healing. If you are a woman, how healthy is the masculine within your feminine essence? Do you trust it? Will you allow it to guide you out into the world of possibilities? Will you allow it to teach you how to initiate, guide, and orchestrate when expressing sexually with your lover?

At this moment, what is your relationship with the blocked energy of shame? What is your relationship with the Divine Masculine and Divine Feminine?

When the flow of masculine and feminine energies stops, people can become trapped, in a sense, in the energetic qualities that are strongest in them. Typically, men become trapped in masculine energies and women become trapped in feminine energies. If people don't know how to connect with their spiritual essence—to relate to the divine model of perfect energy flow—they can become addicted to an imbalanced and broken energy flow.

Unbridled masculine energy that will not enter the feminine leaves the world broken. Unconscious feminine energy that won't draw the masculine to it leaves the world numb. For the flow of masculine and feminine energies to be healthy, it must be complete and unbroken. The feminine energy in men and women must feel safe to receive the goals and confidence of the masculine mind so it can determine if the goals are appropriate for creating and sustaining love, life, and peace. If they are not suitable, the masculine goals must be redirected to come into alignment with the feminine.

Learning how to implement the techniques and suggestions in this book has greatly facilitated the healing of the masculine and feminine energies within and between people who have sought and achieved sexual enlightenment in workshops and private sessions.

Notes: Chapter 8—Third Enlightened Expression—Embrace Masculine Sexual Energy

[1]Deida, *Intimate Communion*, 1995.

.ᵒ 9 ᵒ.

ADDICTION

*D*uring my retreats in the desert wilderness, I offered up sincere words of praise and thankfulness. Equally as important, I asked for and received vital guidance.

Listening to the birds, I can sense the other animals in the bush to my left. I drink water from the belly of my beloved Earth and begin to speak slowly, reverently: "I am grateful for the miracle of life. Thank you for purifying me, cleansing me. Let my mind become one with your spirit. Guide me. Teach me the easiest path, the path of least resistance that leads me to the nameless Thing I honor, whose Will I want to become."

"My Lady, I am drawn to the sweetness of foods to help fill the hollow place that refuses to be filled. But when you are with me, my Lady, the sweetness is created. When I become you—when I feel our union—I feel full. Come to me Mother. Come to me, my Lady. Fill me. I am longing for communion and wholeness."

I continue to expand my awareness by breathing fully and deeply. Instantly, I feel my Lady beginning to communicate with me through my love for Her and Earth. "Honoring your relationship with Me means honoring your relationship with yourself. When you eat food instead of facing consciousness, you are hiding, Little One."

I am humbly communing with Earth and my Lady as I share feelings about my deep emotional need to consume certain foods, especially refined carbohydrates. The need to use food to fill the emptiness, the void, is an attempt to avoid the lack of meaning I experienced in my culture—a hauntingly vague, but persistent lack of being grounded in the physical world, of not feeling planted in the womb of Earth. I feel lost.

—An Excerpt from the Author's Academic Thesis

For Your Consideration: Do you feel a void in your life? What do you do to fill that void? Is it a healthy pursuit? Does it work for you or against you? Becoming conscious of a deep void in your life may be as difficult as becoming conscious of destructive shame in your life. However, both are critically important to acknowledge.

Increasingly, the word "addiction" is being used worldwide to describe serious problems in the civilized and natural world. But what does addiction mean?

Addiction is an outgrowth of trauma, an attempt to avoid confronting pain that lies at the core of a traumatic experience; "trauma is the freeway to addiction."[1] Thus, addiction has a devastating aspect—an out-of-control, often aimless compulsion to replace the lost sense of meaning, honor, and belonging with substitutes such as pornography, drugs, alcohol, consumerism, and food. An addicted person tries desperately to satisfy real and important needs, but because either the external situation or the internal climate does not allow for satisfaction, he or she resorts to less appropriate sources.

This crippling compulsion is then protected from awareness by denial. The addicted person pretends that everything is normal and refuses to admit pain or vulnerability. Addiction then becomes a path of decreasing choices supported by denial, and the person's behaviors, feelings, assumptions, and lack of spirit advance down a path of living that is progressively death-oriented.[2]

The qualities of addiction are sustained and augmented by a person's attraction to repeated trauma. The traumatized person permeates her or his reality with the emotional content of the traumatizing experience, continually reenacting the themes of trauma in order to create the chance to find resolution. However, it rarely works.[3]

Furthermore, the evidence of compulsion, denial, and complete obsession found in personal addiction is not difficult to discover in society at large. The symptoms of addiction are all around us. These kinds of feelings and experiences may have resulted from a cultural pathology: addiction in some form is the natural consequence of humankind's alienation from nature

Some people believe that in one form or another, addiction characterizes every aspect of industrial society.[4] Because of the expansion of scientific knowledge and technological inventions, progress has come to be measured by constant change and novelty, not necessarily by human improvement and continuity.[5]

Arguably, we have become addicted to technology, a human condition that may have guided social development since our departure from our nature-based roots some ten thousand years ago.[6] Therefore, civilization is addicted to the consumption of Earth itself.[7] We have broken some important bonds of life with Earth. Most of our species have forgotten how it feels to be bonded with Earth. More tragically, most fail to remember that they have forgotten. We are increasingly learning that a traumatized state is the very foundation of the domesticated human species.

For us to heal ourselves of current psychological and physical disease, we must address not only the problems that stem from experiences in our own individual lives, but also the deep, chronic, collective problems that manifest themselves in each of us.[8, 9, 10, 11]

Overeating—uncontrollable food consumption that isn't caused by actual hunger, but rather by a person's chronic starvation for real living[12]—is a feminine energy form of addiction. Pornography and other sexual obsessions that cause an uncontrollable release of sexual energy—not because the experience is meaningful, but because the person is chronically searching for deep meaning—are a masculine energy form of addiction. Both of these responses to the unhealthy conditions in our environment are a result of a blocked flow of masculine and feminine energies within and between people, especially in relation to the Divine Masculine and Divine Feminine.

Addictions to Primal Energy

The pelvic floor area of the body around the genitals and anus enables us to feel primal energy—the need for food, air, water, and shelter. The purpose of primal energy is to keep us alive. It gives us our instincts to live. It shouts: "I am alive. I want to live. I want to stay alive." Primal energy doesn't help us understand why we are alive; it only makes us want to do anything possible to stay alive. A person could be having a wonderful spiritual epiphany or listening to exciting music, for example, and be instantly interrupted by a frightening earthquake or a robber wielding a gun. Immediately, primal energy would scream to the person that he or she must do anything to survive, to stay alive, and everything else would be forgotten. Such is the lifesaving function of primal energy.

Furthermore, primal sexual energy is equally as impersonal and powerful as masculine sexual energy because it creates an intensely powerful need to have sex. The impersonal and neutral sex drive wants immediate satisfaction, and it is not greatly concerned about how or with whom it is accomplished. It is simply an intense need to raise and release sexual intensity. Life would definitely not perpetuate itself if primal life force was not present.

Primal sexual energy, or lust, can be a very wonderful, positive, and highly charged energy. Though the energy is impersonal, it can definitely be expressed in a personal way; in other words, with a sacred partner. A person who has never felt this intense, unbridled sexual desire is limited in the kinds of sexual expressions he or she is capable of experiencing. The profound pleasure and erotic intensity of the sexual desire for an intimate partner can be overwhelming. In this context, we learn to relate to, express, and enjoy the wild and tumultuous nature of Earth, which provides an astounding glimpse of the power of Earth's volcanic eruptions and earthquakes! It also helps us better understand the power of the divine. Embracing the beautiful or strong body of a sacred partner and experiencing intense feelings of primal sexual energy are spiritually and sexually healthy occurrences that help us understand, in a small way, the power of eternal creation.

The excitement of lust can also be expressed in an impersonal way with a person who is not necessarily known or cared about; in other words, through a casual sexual experience. In this experience, both the person and the body are objectified. When impersonal primal sexual energy is combined with an impersonal expression, especially through sexually explicit pictures or videos—pornography—the experience can become problematic and even eventually lead to danger or tragedy.

Why? Because the purpose of primal energy is to keep us alive. Typically, we don't think about our primal energy. It automatically and constantly flows through us, reminding us to stay alive and that we need water, food, air, and shelter. However, we can train our primal energy to believe that in addition to needing water, food, air, and shelter to stay alive, we need impersonal sexual experiences, or lust.

Obviously, we don't need lust to stay alive, but the need for it can be equated with the energy of essential primal needs. When this happens, lust begins to consume the consciousness of an individual just as the need for oxygen or food does. The need to have sex as often as possible can become obsessive in nature; moreover, pornography and other impersonal sexual experiences based on primal sexual energy can keep us stuck in lust. It can become so demanding and powerful that we become addicted, in a sense. Primal sexual energy addictions are very difficult to break and can cause horrific results: job terminations, health problems, ruined relationships, and lost lives. Few people understand the power of primal sexual energy and its connection to impersonal sexual experiences. For example, some think they can watch pornography a few times and that will be enough; however, they are playing a dangerous game.

For Your Consideration: At this moment, what is your relationship with your primal sexual energy? What is your relationship with destructive shame? What is your relationship with your deity?

❦

Are you addicted to or obsessed with your primal sexual energy? If the thought of not experiencing sexual energy or having intercourse as often as you like is extremely difficult for you, you may be. In which case, you are running around in circles and becoming impotent when it comes to experiencing the personal transformation that enables you to sense the greater meaning of life. This applies to everyone, no matter how powerful or content a person might think he or she is.

Usually, men who have addictions to primal sexual energy have strong, full, and highly masculine energy cores. As a group, they are confident and strong leaders—motivated, focused, and successful men. Their sexual energies are strong and will be felt often, if not continually, throughout the day. Though pleasant, this can be distracting and even disturbing. Sadly, these men hide this alarming secret from their friends and partners, which only adds to their frustration and anxiety. In addition, if they rely strongly on using their sexual energy to release emotional, spiritual, physical, and mental tension, then their addiction to primal sexual energy intensifies.

What these men do not understand is that their vibrant, expanded, and highly masculine energy cores are full of an impersonal, neutral life force and, therefore, full of impersonal sexual energy. Their road to peace and sexual enlightenment begins when they commit to learn how to transmute sexual energy—to personalize it—and how and when to merge it with love and divine will. If these men learn and use the spiritual tools offered in this book, they have the opportunity to travel a powerful road to health. Hopefully, if they are in relationships, they will be graced with the wisdom, patience, and love of their beloved partners.

Both people would do well to embrace the personal qualities that facilitate a successful journey to sexual enlightenment: be present and conscious in the moment; have faith in the goodness and possibilities of life; acknowledge fear, release it, and open up to love; embrace and honor the common ground of all beings; believe in ecstasy; freely express appreciation; witness and acknowledge daily miracles; be humble, open-minded, and teachable.

The remaining chapters of this book focus on spiritual tools and philosophies that help us personalize and spiritualize our sexual energy. These teachings offer a powerful opportunity for people to potentially release themselves from obsessions with and addictions to primal sexual energy.

Notes: Chapter 9—Addiction

[1]Kellogg, "The Roots of Addiction," 1991.
[2]Wilson Shaef, *Co-Dependence*, 1986.
[3]Kardiner, *The Traumatic Neurosis of War*, 1941.

[4]Berman, *The Reenchantment of the World*, 1981.

[5]Mumford, "The Case Against Modern Architecture," 1962.

[6]Glendenning, *My Name Is Chellis and I Am in Recovery from Western Civilization*, 1994.

[7]Gore, *Earth in the Balance*, 1992.

[8]Berman, *The Reenchantment of the World*, 1981.

[9]Bateson, *Steps to an Ecology of Mind*, 1972.

[10]Mumford, *Technics and Human Development*, 1966.

[11]Hahnemann, *The Chronic Disease*, 1975.

[12]LaChapelle, *Sacred Land, Sacred Sex, Rapture of the Deep: Concerning Deep Ecology and Celebrating Life*, 1988.

✸ 10 ✸
Fourth Enlightened Expression —
Embrace Feminine Sexual Energy

*T*he fourth enlightened expression of sexual energy is symbolized by the area of the heart and chest. The heart is a universal symbol of love and emotions, and therefore, a symbol of the feminine in both men and women. Physically, the heart is protected inside the chest by the ribs. Emotionally, when the feminine heart feels safe and protected, it is willing to open up to love and adoration from itself and others. Thus, the fourth enlightened expression offers men and women the awareness of emotions and love when they are feeling sexual energy.

Let's review the nature of the feminine in men and women, which is present in all life. Typically, women carry considerably more feminine energy than men, so they reveal the following qualities in varying degrees. Women are conscious of aesthetics; they have a love of beauty both inside and outside the body. They are aware of and draw personal relationships to themselves. They recognize and relate to their inner emotions, the energy flow that helps them recognize how they feel about what is happening in the body, in the environment, and in all life around them. The feminine is love.

A woman's body draws and receives ideas, focus, and strength from the masculine mind. Her feminine heart spiritually opens up to and receives his consciousness and direction; sexually opens up to and receives his body; and emotionally opens up to and receives his heart. In the feminine sexual experience, the heart and genitals are connected. Her body wants to be filled with him because she adores him. The beauty of life is at the core of her sexual experience. When she is feeling sexual energy, she intuitively wants to feel the radiance of the Earth in her body.

The divine gift of life, the neutral and impersonal force, is available to every living thing on Earth and in the cosmos. When life energy flows throughout the human body, it is typically felt most powerfully in the genitals. We have the opportunity to choose how to focus this sacred life force that we call sexual energy. It can be used in many ways—positively or negatively, creatively or destructively.

When we express impersonal sexual energy with the heart's consciousness, the experience and expression become very personal. Feminine energy helps us feel and express sexual energy in a loving, erotic, and intimate manner. In a sense, there is no separation between sexual energy and emotions. For example, a deeply feminine woman's love for her partner and ability to open her heart and feelings are wrapped up in her sexual energy. Her emotions and sexual expressions are immensely personal, private, and intimate. Being sexually interested, available, and fulfilled is usually more complicated for a woman than a man.

Typically, a woman needs to feel safe and aware. Her feelings for her partner need to be positive and accepting. Opening up emotionally is difficult for her when she feels angry, resentful, or negative. She needs to feel beauty in her mind, heart, and body. Without her sense of inner and outer beauty, her feminine energy is not fully conscious or healthy. Her body image needs to be positive so she can joyfully experience nudity without shame and repression. She wants her partner to witness the beauty of life as it flows through her. She is aware of her body, knows what it wants and needs, and uses her inner masculine to state those needs in a positive manner. Lastly and most importantly, she wants to feel the beauty of the Divine Feminine within her.

Consequently, a feminine woman is willing to express sexual energy and receive her partner because she wants to relate to her beloved. Conversely, a masculine man will relate to his beloved because his goal is to express sexual energy and release into her. However, a man can learn about sexual love from his own inner feminine, and especially by watching his partner share her body, love, emotions, and sexual energy as she receives him. This kind of learning opens the world of intimate possibilities to him.

A man who naturally carries a high amount of masculine energy can feel driven by the impersonal sexual energy that is part of his predominantly masculine energy core or essence. His naturally impersonal sex drive can be distracting, confusing, and, in the extreme, disheartening and destructive. Finding his inner feminine is critically important for him because he must learn to personalize his sexual expression in order to experience peace, tenderness, love, and intimacy when being sexual—and in his life in general. It is because of his inner feminine that he learns about the essential, influential effect of inner and outer beauty.

This discovery produces a healthy flow of a man's masculine and feminine energies. His feminine partner strives to be physically, emotionally, mentally, and spiritually healthy in her sexuality. She is not only his lover, but is also an example and teacher who helps him learn how to do more than initiate. He learns to open his feminine heart, the home of love and beauty's magnificence. Tender beauty is the radiant light that reveals his and the world's deepest truths.

For Your Consideration: A revered relationship with beauty is absolutely necessary for creating personal and planetary peace. Have you realized the importance of beauty in the world? Is beauty your teacher? How does it teach? What have you learned?

My horse, Sager, is my teacher. When he moves his body, he reveals exquisitely organized form, balance, and continuity. His equine body is an expression of one efficient mass of total logic. However, I doubt that he understands his own brilliant organization of elements. He is not logical or rational in the way that I am. He doesn't know how to read and write; he doesn't speak English or any human language. However, he knows what I don't know. He knows what I want him to do before I request it physically or verbally. Part of my work with him requires that he respond to my physical impulses or sounds. For me, they are more reliable than communicating psychically simply because I don't read his bodymind as well as he reads mine. He knows what I want him to do even before I do.

In so many ways, he is brighter then I am.

Deep communication occurs between us although words are not the best form. We don't share a common consciousness that I perceive. Last night, I was aware enough to meet him in a place common to both of us. It was an experience that was not logical and it could not be measured or defined, yet it magically and magnificently transformed my life.

Sager, they say you are an Anglo-Arab. They say you are powerful, beautiful, fast, sensitive, and eager to learn. They say you are an intelligent horse, a one-person horse. But, my friend, who are you really?

Was it you I felt tonight? Was it you who became me? Was it you who shared the wind with me and listened to the sounds of the night? Was it you — the sound of freedom, the sound of the Mystery?

It was you. I know.

Tonight I didn't take charge the way you allow me during the day. I didn't tell you what to do to define the moment. Instead, I calmly listened and felt. Everything was so quiet and still, the way it always is out there in the Arabian Desert, where only the cats were moving in the middle of the hot night.

They watched us, didn't they, Sager? The other "horses" watched. They knew. They knew that for a few timeless moments we crossed the barriers. Yes, I could see your form. I could feel your soft coat. I could smell you the way I always do. But this time, it all occurred in my heart, a place that energetically became as spacious as the universe. I could not feel my body. In my spaciousness I could hear your intelligence, your power, your intensity. No matter how far away you walked from me, you were still in my heart/body space—pulsating, pulsating, pulsating. My heart opened and became a beacon of light. It was no longer only mine; it was yours, too.

We were the white sand, the quiet breeze, the distant dunes, the Persian Gulf, and the lurking wild cats. We were silence and the shadows that speak so intensely at night.

Sager, they say that you are a horse and I am a human being. They say that we are what we see. They say that there is a barrier between us when we touch, that we "stop." Tonight, neither of us "stopped." We continued. We were each other.

Now, I will never be the same. You, who are so brilliant and observant. You are what sages and saints long to find—in service, yet free.

Someday, my exquisite friend, I will leave you and this desert land of Saudi Arabia and never see you again. When I do, I fear my heart may break. But, I will always carry you and our moments of divinity with me. All I had to do was wait for you, listen, breathe, and open my heart. All I had to do was believe. You are astoundingly beautiful and powerful, my friend.

Sager, because we are one, does that mean I am magnificent and beautiful, too? Yes, I, too, am magnificent and beautiful. But, will I always remember the truth we found, or will I shrink back into my self-consciousness?

Even though I may forget my magnificence and beauty, even though I may forget who I am, even though I may stop loving myself, I will never forget you! If I do forget who I am—and it may happen over and over—it will be the memory of us that will save me. All I have to do is remember you, and

I will remember me. Beauty will save me. You will save me.
Thank you, Sager, my exquisite teacher.
— An Excerpt from the Author's Journal

The fine, priceless communication between a human and a horse is a form of beauty. In its myriad forms, the feminine quality of beauty gives birth to and sustains the human heart of love. Therefore, beauty saves the world from despair. When humans and beauty conceive, rapture is born, which leads to the Creator of Love. Beauty and its infinite manifestations are life loving itself—autumn's silent scent, ecstasy's primal scream, the body's final breath. But, moreover, it is the cornerstone of lovers' tender longing for union.

***

For Your Consideration: Which personal traits could help you
open up to and receive the beauty that lives in your heart?

***

The feminine within men and women enables the beauty of
life—even when it isn't pretty—to swell and open the heart
of love. What do you think about your inner beauty? How
does it feel? This question can sometimes be very painful to
answer, especially for women. Take the time you need to slowly
dive into the depths of your watery truth. If it is painful for you,
courageously wrap your heart around shame—the imprisoned
illusion. Dare to love it enough to set it free.

When the Feminine Stops the Flow of Energies

The energetic cycle of masculine and feminine energies stops when the feminine in men and women will not open up or receive. This creates tension in and between people, and it can cause disharmony, disinterest, or dysfunction.

In Her: There are many reasons why a woman will not open up to or receive her partner. In general, it may not seem appropriate for her, or she may not feel safe. As a result, she will not draw him to her. She may feel emotionally disinterested in her partner because he may not be focused, directed, or strong. Or, she may believe that he is too focused or that his goals are not grounded in truth and love. She may no longer respect or honor him.

Some women allow their essence to grow cold. They may appear to be feminine, but are not emotionally open to men. Because their inner masculine is willful, unhealthy, and out of balance, some women feel highly competitive with men. They may be angry with men in general. Unfortunately, they have learned to distrust the masculine in all men. There is a significant difference between a woman who uses her masculine to move out of her feminine essence and a woman who allows her masculine to help her nurture and live within her healthy feminine essence.

On the other hand, a woman's disinterest in being sexually, emotionally, or physically intimate may have to do with something else. She may be trapped in her own negative feelings and unable to feel her beauty, inside or out. She may not feel good about her body, thinking it is too heavy or thin, and as a result she is embarrassed or ashamed to reveal it. She may be sad and frightened. She may be tired or physically unhealthy. Her hormones may be out of balance. If she has experienced emotional, physical, or sexual trauma, she may not feel safe in her own body. In any of these scenarios, she doesn't feel safe being vulnerable and sexual with her partner. She is full of toxic shame.

If a woman doesn't understand her feminine and what is needed to come back into balance, her state can become a habit. Furthermore, if she won't open to the masculine in her partner, or if her own masculine is weak or wounded, she can become addicted, in a sense, to filling her heart, mind, and body with something that causes her to stay unbalanced and out of her feminine essence.

In order to heal, a woman must learn to reconnect with her spiritual essence. She needs to learn to identify with and believe in her ability to love, to feel beauty inside and around her, and to become intimate with her own warmth and emotional flow. She must witness herself with adoration and receive herself with love. She needs to remember, and desire to express once again, the flow of her feminine essence. She must be willing to open her arms, her belly, her mouth, her legs, and her sacred space to herself. Furthermore, she has to believe that her deity wants her to find that kind of health and peace again.

Finding her essence again may seem impossible, but it is not. It will take time and tremendous effort, faith, and self-love. She must remember that her feminine essence and the fullness of whom she is as a woman are real; the mystery of her femininity is something to be explored and discovered. To be whole and healed, she must learn to feel her Divine Feminine within.

If a woman doesn't feel attractive inside and out, she is not identifying with her Divine Feminine. If she is not safely receiving life, she is not in her sacred feminine. If she does not trust that she is safe to open up and receive, she will close. If she closes, she cannot feel divinity around and in her, and therefore, she cannot receive guidance and direction. She stops her own flow.

A woman is not just feminine, she is masculine too. She must open up to and receive her healthy masculine so she can awaken to her fullness. Without it, she remains unconscious. She is passive and inert, just like an ovum that loses its life force and is no longer capable of creating the flow of life's possibilities when a sperm does not enter it.

It is important for a woman to trust the Divine Masculine within herself. However, when the energy flow stops and she is filled with pain and loneliness, she must admit how much she longs to feel full of love and life, and she will then be ready for the journey into her center, her wholeness. Healing can occur because she learns to relate to and use her divine life force—that she feels as sexual energy—to unite with her spiritual center. Her divine masculine energies can move her out of the emotional pain and into the creation of a new life.

For Your Consideration: If the above ideas have intense meaning for you, breathe deeply using the Breath of Life technique. Allow sounds to flow. Use your tools for shifting insights to help you become more conscious. Ask for divine guidance. If shame is present, strive to release it. Record your responses in your journal.

In Him: A woman who will not open up to her partner creates severe imbalance between them. He will continually try to guide her into an opening and softening of the heart. The longer he tries unsuccessfully, the more unbalanced his energy flow will become. Eventually, he will find it difficult to stay focused on his responsibilities. He may begin to lose focus on his career. He may become angry, frustrated, withdrawn, or even depressed. As a result, he will begin to redirect his attention and interest, intensifying the serious and potentially dangerous imbalance between them. He may find himself trying to reinvent the flow of energy with another woman or with other pleasures—work, career, drugs, alcohol, or anything he can release his energy into—in order to feel warm and peaceful, cared about, or loved. He will certainly do this if his own feminine is weak or unconscious.

If he wants, he can take the journey into his own feminine and masculine energies, his essence, and begin to relate to the Divine Feminine. It is a deep and full journey, one that takes patience, time, and energy. However, if he chooses to take the journey, the possibilities are endless. He can initiate contact with the sacred place in his soul where the Divine Feminine lives; a place full of eternal love for him. The divine being can help him create a flow of life that will always be with him, no matter what happens in the outside world with his partner. With the help of his inner Divine Feminine, he can find his center. His journey may take a few days, months, or an entire lifetime.

The spiritual nature of sexuality becomes his guide. The healing works because he learns to relate to and use his divine life force—that he feels as sexual energy—to unite with his spiritual center. Instead of taking his sexual energy out into the world, he takes it into his own heart; his own Divine Feminine where he finds love and peace.

For Your Consideration: If the above ideas have intense meaning for you, breathe using the Breath of Life technique. Use your tools for shifting insights to help you become more conscious. Ask for divine guidance. Release shame. Record your experiences.

THIRD SPIRITUAL TOOL — MERGE SEXUAL ENERGY WITH LOVE ENERGY

An important and necessary step of the journey to sexual enlightenment is learning how to merge sexual energy with love energy. I have taught this spiritual tool, which can be learned in private sessions or workshops, to numerous clients. Regardless of the factors driving their exploration—from women who wanted to reconnect with their feminine essences to men who wanted to feel and exhibit confidence, focus, and strength in the world—this technique helped them personalize their neutral sexual energy. For example, clients who were practicing celibacy learned to unite their inner masculine and feminine energies with the divine, while those in the winters of their lives felt empowered to peacefully embrace the past and present in preparation for passing. Even government and business leaders utilized this technique to apply their powerful inner energies to living more deeply from a foundation of integrity and honorable purpose.

The following exercise will help you learn to merge sexual energy with love energy so you can personalize your neutral sexual energy. Before beginning this exercise, review and practice the Breath of Life technique found in Chapter 5. In order to practice merging sexual energy with love energy (transmutation), sexual energy must be flowing, which can be achieved with the help of a partner or through self-pleasuring (different from masturbation).

While masturbation and transmutation both involve the use of sexual energy, they are profoundly different and shouldn't be confused. Therefore, a clarification is important. Masturbation—a sexual experience resulting from the use of impersonal, primal sexual energy—can be a highly pleasurable experience. It is also a form of spiritually unprotected sex and a practice that can lead to sexual obsession, sexual addiction, and other serious problems. Masturbation—a sexual technique—reinforces the consciousness of separateness.

On the other hand, transmutation—a spiritual tool—reinforces the consciousness of wholeness. This spiritual experience is created by merging primal sexual energy with divine energy by self-pleasuring and praying or meditating. The highly pleasurable experience that can lead to spiritual ecstasy, inspiration, and personal revelation is spiritually protected sex because of the conscious relationship with deity. Therefore, the experience can never lead to sexual obsession, sexual addiction, or other serious problems. Furthermore, the spiritual tool is more effective than any other approach for releasing people from sexual obsession and addiction.

☙ STEP ONE: Create a sacred space. Candles, gentle music, flowers, oils, and bathing can help create reverence. In addition, prayer and meditation affirm your noble intention to merge neutral sexual energy with love energy—the feminine sexual experience.

Breathe deeply and slowly for several minutes using the Breath of Life technique. This will help release tension and blocked energy in the body so your emotions can flow freely.

 STEP Two: Practice feeling the energy of love—an emotional openness in the chest that enables you to receive and adore someone or something you highly value such as family, friends, children, animals, music, nature, art, a partner, etc. Be willing to feel the energy of your love and adoration expanding in your chest. Experience it until your heart is full and overflowing (grateful tears may be released). Beauty and appreciation are forms of love. Expand your love muscles as much as you can by simply giving yourself the opportunity to be quiet, calm, open, and receptive. Finish step two by using the Breath of Life technique.

Please note: In teaching thousands of people how to merge sexual energy with love energy, I have never met a person who could not feel something they love. When given the chance, it was easy for them to feel their energy cores pulsating with love in their chests.

 STEP THREE: Now concentrate on your entire body. Begin with gentle and slow touching. Next, allow yourself to feel sexual energy by lightly stimulating your genitals. Lovingly touch your whole body or have your partner touch you for several minutes— oil is a great item to use during this time. Afterward, discontinue the touching and breathe deeply and fully several times using the Breath of Life technique.

Remember, one purpose of sexual energy is to understand you have a divinely created energy core running up and down your spine—you know it is true because you feel the intense, pleasure-filled energy in your genitals. However, the goal in stimulating the genitals is to feel small amounts of sexual energy, not to create orgasm or intimacy with another. Simply feel your sexual energy and remember it is a divine gift of life. You are learning to relate your sexual energy to the love you feel for a person or object—not to the person or object itself. In other words, you are not sexualizing the person or object.

✒ STEP FOUR: Repeat steps 1–3.

✒ STEP FIVE: You are now ready to merge love energy and sexual energy. This is done by first creating sexual energy. Do not raise your sexual energy too high or you will not be able to successfully merge the two energies (merging strong sexual energy with love energy takes considerably more practice and concentration). Simply raise sexual energy gently.

While your sexual energy is flowing, receive love energy into your body by feeling the kind of adoration and gratefulness you experienced earlier. Allow the two energies to merge. Remember to relate your sexual energy to the feeling of love you felt for the person or object, not to the person or object—there is a big difference between these two. Also, experiencing these merged energies is completely different from separately experiencing them. Before your sexual energy becomes too intense, stop the touching and just breathe, using the Breath of Life technique.

Rest and allow gratitude to awaken. Remember the source of your sexual energy.

✒ ———————————————————— ☙

For Your Consideration: If you do not have a partner or are choosing celibacy, practice this technique with the understanding that there are many natural gifts of sexual energy and the enlightened expressions of sexual energy are applied at different times for different people. Make a record of your experiences. They will change and evolve. Each time your practice will most certainly be a different experience.

❦

If you are sexually active, this technique will probably be more difficult for you than if you aren't sexually active because you will be used to relating your energy to another person. However, now you will be focusing your energy in a new direction. For example, when you practice, pay attention to the experience of relating sexual energy to the feelings of love rather than to a person you love. Learning to be flexible with your sexual energy prepares you for the experience of relating sexual energy to the divine.

◦ 11 ◦

FIFTH ENLIGHTENED EXPRESSION —
COMMUNICATE SEXUAL TRUTH

*T*he fifth enlightened expression of sexual energy is symbolized by the throat. We are aware of and fully comfortable with communicating our sexual feelings, desires, needs, and emotions. Our partners know they are responsible for their own pleasure; therefore, they listen to their bodies and communicate their personal needs in constructive ways.

Equally as important is our ability and willingness to receive or listen to the personal sexual truth of our partners. Giving and receiving sexual communication is a flow of energy as natural as the mutual giving and receiving of an ocean wave and sandy beach. Love, pleasure, and intimacy deepen as partners give and receive sexual truth. Giving and receiving are essential for successful and healthy relationships of any kind, whether sexual or platonic.

Learning to communicate is a lifelong adventure. Small babies learn to communicate when they laugh, vocalize, cry, or move their bodies. They also receive information from others who hold, touch, vocalize and speak to them. Babies could not thrive without this communication. It can be exciting and deeply meaningful for babies and their loved ones or caregivers to experience this developmental process. Eventually, young children learn to speak in words and sentences—a process highly motivated by the desire to share thoughts, feelings, needs, and wants. They also want to listen to those around them.

It is important to acknowledge and then remember that, in varying degrees, learning to articulate and communicate will continue throughout our lives. The process of effectively expressing thoughts and feelings, as well as listening to the thoughts and feelings of others, is especially valued by people who want to fully engage in positive relationships in a creative life. Doing so reflects the deep need within the human psyche to be understood and valued, to be witnessed.

Effective communication is an essential part of relating to others. We learn to constructively balance our ability to give and receive personal truth—to articulate and communicate well—because we are aware of our inner feelings (feminine) and thoughts (masculine). We understand and honor our essence and unique configuration of life energies within the core of the body. As this happens and depending on our spiritual practices, our feelings, thoughts, and intentions will be expressed in ways that complement and enliven our natural, spiritual essence.

Typically, a female expresses herself from her feminine core; speaking and communicating differently than a male. She is aware of many things happening at once, and her awareness is diffused. For example, she may simultaneously be aware of and try to interpret both her feelings and thoughts as she speaks. She may be feeling her body and the sensations it creates. She speaks her truth from this state of awareness. Therefore, the route to her truth is more complicated and less direct.

Generally, a male expresses himself from his masculine core; communicating less emotionally and more directly and intellectually than a female. He is focused on the experience of his perception and logic. He is aware of goals and the need to communicate and solve problems.

Remembering these basic gender differences will help us establish effective communication patterns, whether we're discussing money, children, spirituality, politics, family, church, work, aesthetics, hobbies, or sex.

For Your Consideration: Do you speak your truth effectively by sharing your thoughts and feelings? Can you say what you need and want with ease? Do you believe you have a right to do so? If you have difficulty, what is the reason?

Do you want others around you to do the same? Do you believe they have a right to their own opinions, regardless of age? How well do you listen?

Do you communicate with your deity? Does your deity communicate with you?

COMMUNICATION IS ESSENTIAL FOR
HEALTHY SEXUAL EXPRESSION

Sexual communication is no less important than any other kind of communication. Sadly, however, it is typically the weakest and most ineffective focus of communication that humans experience. It must not be ignored! Healthy and spiritual sexual expressions depend on it, and so do healthy relationships.

The degree to which people fail to share information when they are sexually intimate is the degree to which boredom, confusion, or even sexual dysfunction develops. This phenomenon occurs because one or both partners are confused about the nature, source, and natural gifts of sexual energy. Few people have been taught the necessary tools for successful sexual intimacy and communication, which poses a serious problem.

Teenagers and young adults who come to workshops are interested in, yet concerned about, the appropriate time for them to make a transition from sexual abstinence to sexual expression. This highly personal choice and responsibility is an important milestone. These young people realize that too much or too little advice, understanding, and education can create confusion. Therefore, their honest and open-minded group discussions about the divine source, nature, and natural gifts of sexual energy are critical. They learn that when the time finally does come for them to fully express themselves sexually, their own wisdom and self-love must accompany them into the sacred celebration or they will become stuck in a sexually obedient or rebellious role.

It is during the critical transition from not being sexually expressive to becoming fully sexually expressive that a confused, unhealthy inner voice tries to convince a person that what is happening in the body and between two mature adults is dangerous, wrong, or immoral. If a person is infected with the energy and sensations that whisper or scream that sexuality is wrong or bad, that the body is ugly, that they do not have the right to say what they want, that the sounds of sex are shameful, or that intense sexual feelings are not natural or spiritual, then that person is having sex with fear.

When sexually intimate people keep their bodies and energies still, hold their breath, close their eyes, shut their mouths, and remain silent—especially during orgasm—it represents reactions to wrong beliefs or inaccurate information. The degree to which a person's physical and energetic body is suppressed or closed at the throat is the degree to which the orgasmic energy is suppressed or closed. Possibilities are silenced. Deep, destructive shame in the soul of a human being is the path to destroying intimacy and love. It locks us into an infantile relationship with our divinely inherited potential. Sadly, it is happening all around us.

However, when both sacred partners are sexually enlightened, they are emotionally open and safe. They know that their divine sexual energies are to be celebrated, and therefore, they have learned that they have the right and the responsibility to communicate about their pleasure, joy, and intimacy. Because they have learned to relate to their sexual energy as divine energy, they are able to appreciate each other and their sexual intimacy in ways that may be impossible to convey through words. Therefore, when they feel love for and loved by their deities while feeling their divine sexual energy, the lovers cry and shout their personal truth for all the heavens to hear. They share the profound expression of their sexual love, their appreciation, and their rapture. They ask for their sexuality, love, devotion, and ecstasy to be heard and witnessed because they are thankful for each other, and they are thankful to be alive! Their loud and joyful orgasmic prayers allow the lovers to speak and listen to their beloved deities.

For Your Consideration: Have you ever been with a lover who was silent? Have you been with a lover who made sexual sounds? Which did you prefer? Which person communicated better?

Are you able to freely make sounds and communicate when intimately and sexually expressive? If not, why? Are you able to communicate with your deity when sexually expressive? Why or why not?

What is your relationship with the illusion of shame at this moment?

Transition into Being Fully Sexual

How do we make a healthy transition from not being sexual to being fully sexual? First, we understand how important it is to focus on that transition. Next, we take into account the circumstances and make adjustments. For example, is a person becoming fully sexual for the first time in his or her life? Is a person returning to being fully sexual after a period of no activity? Is a person fully sexual, but realizes that he or she does not take full responsibility for his or her needs? Perhaps a person realizes that shame or even abuse issues play an important part in his or her inability to communicate well about sexuality. These examples show there are many different ways to learn about and work with the fifth enlightened expression.

For Him: A man's natural sexual experience is not as complicated as a woman's. Obviously, he must feel the need for sexual expression, which is typically more about sexual energy than emotions. We are not suggesting that a man is not emotional when making love, but rather that it is possible for him to stay in his masculine essence and not feel emotionally close to his partner. Such is the nature of masculine sexual energy. The goal of his sexual energy is to release into his partner and into life, to give to his partner so he will be received.

Additionally, a masculine man can become so focused on giving pleasure to his partner that he fails to learn how to truly relax and receive. Extreme masculine focus during sexual activity can cause a man to become preoccupied with thoughts rather than sensations and emotions. He may then become bored and disinterested, and have trouble with premature ejaculation, orgasm, or even maintaining an erection. If this happens, he must learn to feel and communicate better with his partner.

The strength of expressed truth becomes the strength of a couple's orgasmic energy. The conscious use of breath allows the spiritual lovers to give birth to personal truth through sounds.

They understand that their sexual, orgasmic energies feed both the spiritual body and the physical body.

———————————————

For Your Consideration: If couples who demonstrate goodwill understand and remember the significant differences between genders, then their sexual communication can be effective and exciting. Because the fifth enlightened expression opens the door to evolved expressions of sexual energy — the aware-ness of giving and receiving personal truth — they learn to use sexual sounds of pleasure to call to the beloved divine. Do you agree? Why or why not?

If you are a man, when giving pleasure to your lover do you often become so focused on giving that you don't relax and receive well?

Does your partner know how you like to be touched? Do you express your preferences? Do you know how to explore being touched consciously?

———————————————

For Her: Generally, it is more complicated for a feminine woman to be sexually intimate than it is for a man. Being sexually intimate is usually a very personal experience for a woman. She must feel close to her partner, feel her love for him. Her sexual energy and her love for her partner are not separate. She wants to carry a healthy sense of love for her body, to feel beautiful and have a sense of her inner beauty.

She learns to listen to her body and say what she wants in a positive way. Doing so takes practice. Moreover, not only does she have the right to communicate what she needs and wants, but she also has the responsibility to say what she needs and wants. It is vitally important.

Ideally, a woman who loves her partner and wants to be intimate learns to communicate what she needs. She can quickly become disinterested in making love if she doesn't learn to communicate. An emotionally healthy, feminine woman who loves her partner will naturally want to be close physically. She will be receptive to his natural ability to initiate and guide them in their sexual expression. He will feel the need to give to her and bring her pleasure. Though he cannot truly know what she needs, he will have the confidence to try! His tempo, his touch, and his sexual needs may be different at any moment from hers.

If she makes love with him because she adores him and wants to be close, but doesn't say what she wants and needs, she can teach herself to stop listening to her body. If she does that very often, she will teach herself to not be "present" or aware of what is happening in her body, so her physical needs may not be met. This causes tension in her feminine psyche. Before she knows it, she is not nearly as interested in or excited about being sexually expressive. She has allowed the desire to be close to her partner to become more important than the awareness of her physical body. In essence, she has abandoned her own physical and sexual needs for the desire to be close to her man.

Most women create this complicated sexual issue. The problem can occur within only a few days or weeks of becoming sexual with a partner. The sexual issue can persist throughout the relationship or marriage, and if it is not addressed, it will most likely cause great sexual tension between her and her partner.

On the other hand, men often have trouble personalizing their sexual expression. In order for men to learn to personalize their sexual energy they must know how to flow into their own feminine energy or watch and learn from a female partner. If their feminine partner has trouble communicating, then the man has trouble learning. He has to try to read his partner's mind and body. If he is a confident lover, he will assume that he is good at reading her body and mind, and if he doesn't correctly read her, she will become frustrated. And if he is not a confident lover, she will become frustrated. Consequently, it is as important for a feminine partner to learn to communicate as it is for a masculine partner to learn to personalize neutral sexual energy

The next chapter introduces a powerful touch and communication technique called Conscious Touch, which offers partners a method for creating powerful communication.

For Your Consideration: If you are a woman, how good are you at communicating your feelings, sounds, preferences, and thoughts when you are being intimate and sexual? Does your partner know how you like to be touched?

❧❦❧

Not taking responsibility for your sexual needs may be a result of passivity. Are you passive? Why or why not?

Ineffective communication is not just a sexual issue. It is an issue that can exist in every aspect of our lives. Furthermore, it can be a challenge particularly for women because feminine inner meanings, senses, and emotions—indirect and diffused—are not always easily translated into thoughts. They are not masculine meanings—direct, focused, and mental. What an interesting difference in perspective and experience between the natural process of masculine and feminine communication.

By writing in my journal, I first began to articulate my personal struggle with words and meaning when I was a young, single parent.

I remember that October day well. It was the time of Earth's magical cycle when the sun simultaneously wanes and warms. I had just driven the thirty minute reentry zone between the Calgary east side elementary school where I taught as a music specialist and the west side home where I lived as a single parent with my two young daughters.

It was the end of a school day and, as usual, I cried during the drive home—my way of acknowledging fatigue and releasing tension and the energy of others that had invaded me. Needing food, I stopped at my favorite bookstore and quickly scanned the shelves to discover words to feed my hungry mind and resurrect my weary spirit. Instinctively, my hearthand reached for Ken Wilber's No Boundary *and Susan Griffin's* Women and Nature. *Spending my last dollars on a book, some music, or a piece of pottery was a sacrificial ritual I performed whenever I had little money, or felt lonely or exhausted. Beauty always rescued my lovely children and me.*

Rarely would I have time to read books from cover to cover. Often I would not read a single page. But the words had a way of silently oozing from their white beds into mine, making love to me as I slept, filling those empty spaces in my heart, body, and mind, and becoming my lovers and friends. The books I purchased that day contained theories about freedom and liberation for women, for men, for humankind. In theory, I was free and empowered, yet in practice I felt enslaved and exhausted. I longed for a rebirth, but I didn't know how to effectively articulate it — to bridge the emotional and mental gap.

Today, my two precious girls no longer sleep in their little beds in that sweet home in Calgary. Those days are gone forever. Time has taken them to their sweet homes with their own children in their little beds. My daughters have grown into bright, articulate, and sensitive young women. Beautiful women.

Nevertheless, our lives are in sync as usual. We yearn to make our personal visions conscious and embodied, to speak with our own voices in our own words, to give back to the Mystery in our own ways. We laugh and struggle together as usual, helping each other learn to articulate deep meanings, so many of which cannot be explained with words.

—An Excerpt from the Author's Journal

In workshops and private sessions, the fifth enlightened expression of sexual energy is explored in depth. Representing all varieties of race, religion, ethnicity, and sexual orientation, women practice writing and speaking about personal meaning, finding ways to express what they feel is missing in their cultures and everyday lives, and creating new words for expressing nearly extinct experiences. During the workshops, men often watch this sacred, deliberate process of creation with fascination.

Writer, Marilyn Sewell eloquently describes her discomfort with issues of gender and language.

> *Not long ago I discovered that I have no language. Not just me personally, of course, but women. Women have no language.*
>
> *That discovery shook me deeply. It explained perhaps why I often have this sense of muteness, this pulling back from known words and patterns of language, doubling back and redoubling upon myself. But where am I to find a voice? The cultural/lingual patterns were laid in place, solidly, years before I even came into this world, were they not?*
>
> *All writers must be creators, but women writers must create twice: we must re-create our materials—the very words and word patterns of our medium—and at the same time we must create our individual pieces of writing. We have no ready-made system, no vocabulary in place, no easy syntax, no context of allusions, and no given subject matter to embrace us and call us forth.*
>
> *Where can we begin? Perhaps with the silence, the monumental silences; the multitude of feelings and understanding that we have discounted as not real because there has arisen no word, no phrase, no pattern of thinking to legitimize our experience. To remain in these silences is to be alone. There is no way to connect flesh with flesh, no way to perceive, to preserve, to "know." So we fumble with words, playing with*

them, caressing them, trying to tease out meaning. We work as if our lives were at stake. As if life were at stake. And we would be right in supposing so.[1]

Without a doubt, language and gender is a complicated issue. However, to simplify, it can be explained with one word—energy.

The feminine energy in women and men dwells in the land of emotions, beauty, love, the body, and relationships. And if the language of that land seems foreign, there is a good reason. The feminine language is not a thought; it cannot be spoken in words. The feminine language is a feeling in the body. It is expressed through natural sounds: laughing, crying, moaning, groaning, sighing, screaming, growling, and everything in between.

How do we teach the feminine energy in the body to communicate complicated feelings with nouns, verbs, adjectives, and adverbs? Conversely, how do we teach the masculine mind to communicate complicated thoughts with sighs, grunts, moans, and screams? How do we turn apples into carrots? We can't. Why would we want to? Both are to be respected.

We have other alternatives. There is an exciting universal ability that we can consider—the ability to listen.

In the communication process, listening is as equally important as verbalizing (masculine) or sounding (feminine)! Some of us are good at listening to others. Unfortunately, many of us are good at plugging our ears. When we refuse to honor gender differences, we lack goodwill and fight to convince the opposite sex that it is innately wrong.

How can alienated and muted humans who crave union and communication with their bodies, with each other, with Earth, and with the divine learn to listen? Perhaps we begin by believing that we can hear *and* listen.

Our bodies will communicate with us. Respect the fact that our partners are communicating through the energies of their natural energetic essences. Listen to Earth communicate with us in its natural form. If we can communicate thoughts and feelings in our natural forms, why wouldn't our creator communicate with us in its natural form?

If our ears are plugged, why not take out the plugs? Expect to hear miracles, not only in our sexual expressions, but in every aspect of our lives. Remember, our enlightened sexual expressions are metaphors for the communication in our lives. Let others know about our unusual experiences! Listen to them share their miracles!

The following story about communication was a miraculous experience in my life.

Feeling fragile and tender, I sit on the hot, red sand underneath a gangly, sprawling mesquite bush. I focus on my body as I touch and gently rub my legs, my back, and my chest. I struggle to release loneliness from my tender heart.

Suddenly, a small bird quickly flies from silence and lands in the mesquite bush one foot from my face! I am shocked to find such a wild one would come so close to me. But, immediately I understand that the sweet bird has come for a specific reason—she is speaking for the divine. The messenger and I look sharply at each other; our wide and intensely firm eyes acknowledge the sacred directive.

We enter an eternity of silence and breath.

And then, very slowly, the mystical music begins.

We offer each other sounds that bridge the vocal gap. The bird sings to me. I chant to the bird. She responds to me. I call to her. Eyes locked, simultaneously we communicate. In har-

mony, we breathe. Back and forth, back and forth, back and forth—we send and receive the divine message of oneness.

Then, silence and breath.

Finally, she flies.

I soar.

"Thank you my friend. How can I ever feel alone again?" I quickly declare.

—An Excerpt from the Author's Academic Thesis

For Your Consideration: Do you believe in interspecies communication? Why or why not? Sexual longing for union with another is a metaphor for the longing for union with all life. You are not alone.

What communication have you experienced with another species that you would share with someone who would listen respectfully?

Your enlightened sexuality is a metaphor for life—you have the opportunity to create love with all of life. Your comfort with sexual sounds and silence paves the way for intimate communications with Earth's nature and your God. Conversely, intimate communication with Earth's nature and your God paves the way for intimate communication with your sexual lover. You are capable of and responsible for being fully expressive in all aspects of your life. Do you agree with the above ideas? Why or why not?

❧❀☙

Discuss this chapter with others, including members of the opposite sex. Notice how well you are willing to communicate. Are you willing to listen when you don't agree? It is not a debate unless you would rather be right than happy.

❧❀☙

Sound and silence are equally important when communicating. Are you comfortable with silence as well as sounds when talking and listening?

❧❀☙

Practice self-pleasuring and releasing sounds of pleasure and appreciation. State your sacred intention and ask for divine guidance. Create your own sacred celebration.

──────────────────────────

Notes: Chapter 11—Fifth Enlightened Expression—Communicate Sexual Truth

[1]Sewell, *Cries of the Spirit: A Celebration of Women's Spirituality*, 1991, 1.

ᘓ 12 ᘒ

CONSCIOUS TOUCH

*C*onscious Touch, the fifth spiritual tool for creating sexual health, is a highly effective communication tool designed to be used when partners are consciously giving and receiving touch. It is a technique that helps provide safe and appropriate boundaries for a person who is accepting responsibility for the manner in which he or she explores being touched. Therefore, it is a powerful, essential tool for discovering appropriate and healthy expressions of sexual energy no matter what your reasons are for embarking on the astonishing journey to sexual enlightenment.

Participants in both my private sessions and workshops identified this tool as a fundamental key to opening the door to sexual communication—not only when it came to talking about sexuality, but also in being sexually expressive. Whether they were beloved partners who were sexually frustrated and bored or couples who were sexually healthy and satisfied, they all wanted to better understand and communicate with their partners so they could deepen and strengthen their relationships. Some clients were new mothers who wanted to regain a sense of ownership over their bodies so they could reopen to sexual expression, while others were women who longed to know and express what it really means to be a woman in the world today. Some were well educated, innovative sex therapists striving to gain a broader picture of sexual communication so they could offer more effective guidance to their clients. In addition, some globally minded participants had an intense desire to make positive changes in the world and instinctively knew that being able to communicate about human sexuality was a matter of paramount importance.

THE FOUR ELEMENTS OF CONSCIOUS TOUCH

The person receiving touch, the "passive receiver," learns to listen carefully to what his or her body is saying, to feel what is needed and wanted, and then gives specific directions to the person doing the touching, the "active receiver." The passive receiver repeatedly practices giving directions to the active receiver while taking responsibility for communicating when being touched, and doing it in a clear and positive manner. He or she learns to feel empowered and safe.

The active receiver also sets boundaries. He or she has the responsibility to agree or not to agree to do what is being asked. Both people learn to trust that what they say will be honored by the other person—respecting boundaries is critical.

The passive receiver should be sitting or lying down. The active receiver should be standing or sitting. A chair, sofa, or bed is adequate, but a massage table is ideal for practicing conscious touch because it is high enough for the active receiver to be comfortably standing, sitting, and bending.

When practicing conscious touch for the first time, the following four elements are introduced and practiced one at a time. Afterward, all four are practiced simultaneously. One or both partners can be fully dressed or completely undressed, depending on what is appropriate.

ꙮ STEP ONE—MAINTAIN EYE CONTACT: During conscious touch, partners practice maintaining eye contact to create a mentally and emotionally unifying experience. Eye contact creates a keen awareness of what is happening in the moment—the body is being consciously honored, touched, and explored.

Most people are not used to sustaining eye contact and may be shy or even uncomfortable at first. However, eye gazing can be deeply revealing because our eyes tell the truth. A great deal can be discovered when we learn to understand what our partner's eyes are revealing. In many ways, eye contact can be more communicative than words, sounds, or body language.

We begin by looking into each other's eyes without talking or touching for several minutes (or perhaps many minutes). Eye gazing may stir thoughts and emotions between us and our partners. Allow the experience to unfold without talking about it—learn to "feel" the partner's eyes and be comfortable with the silence. Watch the passive receiver carefully. Witness the mysterious and silent language of the eyes. Practice learning it. Eye contact is critical for truth to be witnessed and our consciousness to be expanded.

For Your Consideration: How do you feel about your experience with eye gazing? If you find that your experience was too intense, breathe and allow your throat, chest, neck, and shoulders to relax, then try again.

STEP TWO—BREATH AND SOUND: After we have created a sense of safety and closeness through eye contact, breathing and sounding are introduced. While practicing the second element, the passive receiver is encouraged to breathe and vocalize when being touched. Eventually, partners feel comfortable communicating with sighs, moans, laughter, groans, words, and even crying as ways of allowing the breath to flow fully when the body is being touched. Partners learn to breathe freely when practicing conscious touch so they can readily do the same when sexual energy is flowing.

Breathing and sounding are important for several reasons. The breath feeds the body and allows for energy in the body to flow freely, especially when couples are raising sexual energy. As breathing and sounding release tension, anxiety, and blocked energy, awareness is expanded within and between partners. It is important to know and remember that sounding and breathing greatly intensify orgasmic energy.

In order to practice breathing and sounding, the active receiver begins to touch the passive receiver lightly and softly on the arms while maintaining eye contact. The arms are probably safe to touch until the passive receiver learns to direct the active receiver. Both partners should concentrate on breathing well. While exhaling, quiet sounds can be practiced as a way to remember to breathe and sound.

When the active receiver also breathes and sounds it can help the passive receiver feel comfortable doing the same thing. This part of the technique can release tension. Oftentimes, people smile and laugh at this point because it seems silly or exaggerated. Partners continue to practice for a few minutes until both feel confident and relaxed. A small amount of talking might be justified, but long sentences or lengthy conversations should certainly be avoided. The partners are learning a new kind of communication!

For Your Consideration: Active Receiver, as you touched your partner on the arm were you comfortable feeling him or her? Were you able to touch without trying to direct or control your partner's responses?

Passive Receiver, were you able to trust the touch experience and also maintain eye contact? How did you feel? What was your relationship with your deity?

STEP THREE—GIVE VERBAL DIRECTIONS: The passive receiver is now ready to practice communicating more directly through words and sentences about how he or she wants to be touched. The active receiver starts the activity by first placing and holding the hand on the passive receiver's upper chest, just below the throat. While maintaining eye contact, the passive receiver breathes and prepares to accept the responsibility of directing the touching process.

For women, this can be a very emotional moment, especially for those who have been married and sexual for years because this may be the first time they are taking the opportunity to be completely in charge of their bodies. It is not unusual for a woman to choose to have her partner's hand held on her upper chest for 5 to 10 minutes because she is so overwhelmed by her sense of safety, intimacy, and empowerment. She may feel very emotional when she realizes she is consciously in charge of how she is touched.

When ready, the passive receiver continues the process of directing his or her partner to touch the body in the places he or she wants to be touched. Be specific about speed and pressure, and be open to exploring different ways of being touched: circling, scratching, massaging, etc. Perhaps say something like this: "Try moving your fingers slowly and lightly over my belly." "Hold your hand on my kneecap." "Gently rub up and down my lower arm." Continue the eye gazing, breathing, and sounding.

While the passive receiver gives a direction and receives touch, he or she takes the time to be conscious of what is happening in the body so he or she will know if he or she wants to continue receiving that particular kind of touch and for what duration. The mind won't tell him or her, the body will. Therefore, listen to the body and let it communicate. Always use positive words to communicate with the active receiver. Remember that he or she is not trying to guide the passive receiver. If the active receiver is a man, he will be trying to not use his masculine energy to guide or control his touch. Consequently, it is up to the woman to use her inner masculine energy to direct her partner, understanding that he is learning to trust that she will say what she wants in an honest and positive manner.

Typically, people can be so tender and vulnerable when it comes to giving and receiving touch that one negative comment from their partner can have destructive results. A negative comment can plant the seeds of doubt and shame. It may not be openly or consciously acknowledged at the time, but the effects can be long lasting or even permanent.

The woman is learning to trust her ability to feel her body, explore it through touch, and become empowered by communicating to her partner exactly what she wants. In doing so, she learns to trust the active receiver. She learns that he will touch her exactly how she asks to be touched, not what he thinks would pleasure her, how he would like her to be touched, or how he would like to touch her. He is simply receiving her body into his hands—his hands are actively moving over her body while consciously receiving her, hence the term active receiver.

The man learns to trust that his partner will discover and communicate what interests her. He learns to not always be responsible for how she is touched. In this communication activity, he is not actively initiating the way he normally would during their sexual intimacy. It is important to remember that he will continue to be confident in his ability to initiate and guide her when the two of them are sexually intimate; however, because they have practiced conscious touch, he will also listen to her tell him more clearly what she wants! In addition, she will listen to him do the same thing. Both sacred lovers will know how to initiate and receive. Therefore, boredom and dysfunction have a significantly smaller chance of sneaking into their lovemaking.

For Your Consideration: What is your relationship with your deity at this moment? Were you able to listen to your bodies and to each other while touching, sounding, breathing, and eye gazing? Discuss your experiences with each other.

STEP FOUR — REASSURE: The passive receiver gives feedback so the active receiver knows he or she is doing what is requested (unless they choose to decline the request). Then the active receiver can relax. If the passive receiver is silent, it is nearly impossible for the active receiver to know what his or her partner is feeling or thinking. That is why breathing and sounding are important—they communicate! (The same reasoning is true when sexual energy is felt and flowing.) Tension, confusion, and uncertainty are created if proper feedback is not offered. Therefore, the passive receiver learns to reassure the active receiver with positive feedback. Personalize the comments by using the person's name. For example, say things like: "Yes, that is great Marie." "That is exactly what I wanted Tony." "Perfect. Thank you." If it isn't exactly what was wanted, give more directions and then reassure the active receiver.

Both partners are practicing conscious touch, using it as a communication and exploration tool in a learning activity. It is important to note that although the practice session may raise sexual energy for intimate partners, when practicing this technique, they are not involved in their normal process of sexual expression. In fact, before you start to practice, it is best for partners to agree that intimate sexual expression will not occur during the practice period. Therefore, they are free from intense sexual activity so they can concentrate on learning to better communicate and explore touch. Subsequently, when they are intensely sexual, they can use this new tool for exploring and communicating in profoundly different ways.

During the practice session, partners should maintain eye contact 90 percent of the time. Practicing all four parts separately may last only a few minutes or as long as an hour or more.

For Your Consideration: Passive Receiver, were you conscious and expressive? Ideally, you would use both your masculine and feminine energies well. Practice this step so you feel comfortable.

Active Receiver, were you able to relax and trust your partner's responses to your touch? If not, try it again and ask for reassurance.

COMBINE THE FOUR ELEMENTS OF CONSCIOUS TOUCH: After the elements have been practiced separately, the partners are ready to combine them. While maintaining eye contact, they repeatedly breathe and sound, give verbal directions, and offer reassurance.

The more conscious touch is practiced, the more both partners learn to trust, explore, and communicate effectively. They learn to take responsibility for their separate experiences. The passive receiver learns to take responsibility for having his or her body touched and explored on his or her terms because communication is offered in an honest, conscious, specific, and positive manner. He or she learns to trust that the active receiver will listen to directions without trying to initiate or guide touch. The active receiver learns to trust and relax because he or she knows the passive receiver will communicate in a positive tone.

The possibility of successful, intimate, and healthy exploration through touch is significantly increased if the communication tool of conscious touch is practiced and permanently integrated into sexual intimacy. Remember that typically, boredom, frustration, and eventually dysfunction sets in when partners simply do not know how to communicate or will not take responsibility for communicating. On the other hand, when sexual energy is being expressed and you are intimate, conscious touch should not be used constantly or it can also create boredom and frustration.

For Your Consideration: Partners, when you are comfortable with the communication tool, be adventurous in the exploration of touch!

Passive Receiver, be courageous in your willingness to explore being touched in your sacred places. Find new power spots!

*Allow yourself the freedom to move freely and explore all
parts of your body. Move. Change positions. You are in charge
of the adventure!*

❧❀❧

*Active Receiver, when your partner becomes adventurous in
exploring his or her body, maintain your focus and do not try
to lead the exploration. Enjoy and have fun!*

CONSCIOUS TOUCH FOR CHILDREN

Conscious touch can be used in many contexts, and is appropriate for family, friends, and partners. It is wise and wonderful for children to learn at an early age that they can ask to be touched and that they are in charge of how that happens. Being tickled and rubbed can be delightfully fun and pleasurable! Most important, children must learn that they always have the right to be in charge of how they are touched. However, it is simply not enough to explain this right to children. They learn this concept by practicing it in a happy, safe, and appropriate environment. The fun activity should always be supervised by both parents or two adults. The child would be fully dressed or in a bathing suite. Teach them that during the game of conscious touch, there is no touching in the area of the underwear. These rules help them to learn about healthy boundaries. Consequently they are establishing a foundation for healthy sexuality that they will build upon as adults.

Teach children about these strict rules for receiving touch from anyone at any time:

Rule 1: Children are to tell their parents if anyone of any age insists on touching them without their permission or in ways that don't feel right. This definitely includes all immediate family members, extended family members, baby sitters, and friends.

Rule 2: Children are to tell parents if another person threatens to hurt them or their parents if the child will not do what the threatening person wants.

Teach children these basic safety rules the same way you teach them about traffic, fire, water, drugs, etc. Role-play shouting and screaming so children know what to do without hesitation if a person is threatening or frightening them. Don't assume that they will know what to do if they haven't practiced it—they won't because they are too naïve and vulnerable.

For Your Consideration: What is your relationship with your deity at this moment? If shame is present, use your tools for shifting insights, talk to a trusted adult, and release the illusion of shame.

This topic can be emotional and highly charged with adults for various reasons. Consciousness raising groups can be quite lively when discussing conscious touch. Consider organizing such a group!

CONSCIOUS TOUCH FOR
TEENAGERS AND YOUNG ADULTS

As puberty creates changes in the body, teenagers become more aware of the heightened sexual sensation they probably felt with much less intensity as children. Consequently, it is vitally important for them to continue practicing and learning the tool of conscious touch. It is unhealthy for young adults to be afraid or ashamed of their sexual energy, or to suppress their feelings. Conversely, it is unhealthy for young adults to not have personal boundaries in place regarding sexuality. It is a critical time. They must learn to understand, accept, and relate to this intensely new and natural aspect of being alive.

Teenagers and young adults need tools! They need to be educated! If they do not feel comfortable hearing about and exploring the communication tool of conscious touch in appropriate and fun ways with friends or family members, they should not be exploring physical touch with a significant partner of the opposite sex. Their new and powerful sexual energy may be used unconsciously and in ways that create sexual wounds, emotional problems, deep shame, and life-changing problems in the future. Talking about the concept of taking responsibility for how they are touched is an essential part of learning to be responsible for pleasure and sexual energy.

If teens have been taught as children about the nature, source, and natural gifts of their pleasurable life force and sexual energy, then the foundation for sexual health has been laid. It they weren't taught these as children, then certainly now is the time. Give them this book. Let them read and study it, and discuss it with them thoroughly.

186 • More Than You Ever Imagined

For Your Consideration: If you are a parent of a teenager or young adult, what are your responses to the conscious touch tool? Do you have any concerns that need to be expressed to your son or daughter?

If you are a teenager or young adult, what are your responses to the conscious touch tool? Do you have any concerns that need to be expressed to your parent?

Can you imagine practicing this technique in a positive, fun, and appropriate atmosphere in a sexual education class, social gathering, or other settings? Why or why not?

Can you imagine practicing this technique at a church gathering? Toxic shame will always tell you it is a crazy, bad idea! Be aware of any shame that you might feel when even considering the idea. Are your thoughts and feelings based on personal preferences or deep shame and fear? Have a good time with this topic!

Conscious Touch for
Serious or Engaged Couples

Serious or engaged couples are strongly encouraged to carefully read and study this book. Ideally, before they are fully expressive sexually, couples would know how to be fully expressive emotionally, intellectually, and spiritually regarding sexuality.

Talking about sexuality greatly prepares them for marriage. Emotionally and spiritually healthy couples who are serious or engaged would naturally love to be close physically. They are sexually aroused by each other, and love to hug, kiss, and hold each other close. Furthermore, when they finally choose to be fully sexual, they do it because they believe it is the right thing to do, not because they are afraid of being sexually intimate or not. They are disciplined and sincere in preparing for the wonderful blessings and experiences they will receive through sexual intimacy with each other

If couples cannot talk about sex before they get married, they should delay the marriage until they can. If one or both feel embarrassed or ashamed, a bright red flag is being raised to warn them something is wrong. There are probably serious problems needing to be addressed.

If one or both partners are not sexually attracted to their future spouse, the sexual issue may not disappear after marriage. It is very unwise to commit to sexual fidelity unless both partners are sexually attracted to each other. Take the time to find out what is happening! Practice conscious touch.

Conscious Touch for Newly
Committed or Married Couples

Newly committed or married couples are strongly encouraged to carefully read and study this book both together and separately.

Understanding the nature, source, and natural gifts of sexual energy is the foundation for the eight enlightened expressions of sexual energy. Respecting gender needs and differences is the foundation of a loving sexual relationship or marriage. Honoring the masculine and feminine flow of energy within and between spouses is directly related to honoring the eternal union of the Divine Masculine and Divine Feminine.

Practicing and using the technique of conscious touch will greatly benefit both partners. It is a wise man who understands his feminine partner and her ability to be receptive and guided. If he is sexually educated, he knows her feminine receptivity is naturally more developed than her ability to direct his touch. Consequently, while practicing conscious touch, he will carefully try not to guide her into what he might think is appropriate for her. He knows conscious touch is a skill she is learning that will allow them to be more joyfully intimate and sexual because she will understand and practice her right and responsibility to communicate about what she needs and wants. He encourages her to love listening to her body as much as she loves receiving him. Hence, she will remain fully aware of her body while being touched by him. He encourages her to learn to speak her truth, to tell her story, because he knows it is an important step in learning to fully claim her body as an expression of sexual and sensuous joy.

Oftentimes, a woman will have difficulty being sexually intimate after marriage because before marriage, she told her body "no" in negative and fearful ways too many times. She waited until marriage to be fully sexual because she was afraid and ashamed, not because she thought it was the best thing to do and so joyfully decided to wait. She was negative instead of positive in making choices. She taught her heart and body to feel bad and wrong when being sexual.

Subsequently, learning to consciously say "yes" to the body will most likely take time and practice. It is a critical time for the woman—and a critical time for the marriage! It is a wise couple who understands this sexual issue. They know they must learn some techniques now to allow the sexual energy to flow, to release shame, and to feel free, loving, and beautiful in their sexual expressions. The feminine woman must restore parts of herself that have been scattered, hidden, denied, or forbidden. She begins that process by discovering and sharing personal truths about her feelings, body, and sexual energy.

She must learn to honor her personal tempo and process, to be aware of her emotions and needs when she is being touched. She must understand that not only does she have the privilege of learning to speak her truth when she is sexual, but it is her responsibility to do so. She must learn to honor and listen to her emotions, thoughts, and body's sensations. Then she will want her sacred partner to relate both to her expressed truth and to her willingness to have him guide her in their lovemaking. Most important, she must release her shame and fear. Sometimes, professional help or counseling may be required.

Typically, being sexually intimate is less complicated for a man who is a new partner or husband than for his partner. Since he may not have learned the fourth enlightened expression—he would not know how to personalize his sexual energy. Consequently, though he definitely feels his sexual goals, he is less emotional and complicated in his sexual expressions.

However, he might become so interested in guiding his feminine partner into her sexual pleasure that he doesn't learn how to consciously receive touch or feel his body as well as he would like. His natural interest in setting and obtaining sexual goals might take him away from the fullness of sexual expression. Thus, he must learn to receive the truth of his own body, and then to express that to his partner. Practicing conscious touch helps him learn to relax, to feel his body, and to learn how to direct his partner without allowing his natural masculine impulse to focus on giving her pleasure.

⚙ 13 ⚙

SIXTH ENLIGHTENED EXPRESSION—
WITNESS SEXUAL TRUTH

*T*he sixth enlightened expression of sexual energy is symbolized by the eyes. It teaches us about the combined awareness of spiritual and sexual perception, knowledge, and perceived truth. During sexual intimacy, it is through the consciousness and energy of the eyes and the mind that we discover the vibrant, holy truth of the moment. The experience is profoundly transpersonal. When partners look into each other's eyes, they see the reflection of their humanity. It is through these windows to the soul that partners witness the great power of life flowing in each other when they are emotionally, spiritually, physically, or sexually intimate, and especially during orgasm.

During this unordinary state of consciousness, the focused and directed energy of the mind travels at the speed of thought. In their sexual intimacy and through their eyes, couples momentarily merge with the consciousness of the universe! Simultaneously, they are at home in the human body and the body of the cosmos. When intimate lovers are breathing fully, sounding freely, and gazing on each other during orgasm, they are opening the door to the instant voyage through the heavens, to the home of their gods. Their eyes are watching divine creation.

During an extremely intimate sexual experience, an orgasm not only embodies powerfully rapturous feelings that invigorate and nurture the body, mind, and spirit, but also acknowledges love and the mystical yearning for union with the divine. The orgasmic experience that is witnessed through the power of the eyes is the same consciousness that is created through sincere and reverent prayer, meditation, and communion. This phenomenon occurs when primal sexual energy is consciously changed to spiritual energy.

The perceptive freedom that is available in the minds and eyes during this astoundingly spiritual expression of sexual energy and orgasm is rarely understood until it is experienced and deliberately practiced. By looking into the eyes of their beloved partners—especially during orgasm—couples momentarily enter into the holistic oneness. The perceptive mind explodes into brilliance. The boundaries of the mind are temporarily dissolved as the eyes peer inside the splendor of love and life. For a few eternal moments, lovers experience the mystery of life. They are liberated and enlightened. They are one and all. They are nothing and everything. When vulnerable and emotionally open sacred partners practice this beautiful intensity, they reaffirm their enduring commitment to eternal union. Divinity flows through an honorable man. Divinity flows through a beautiful woman. We are the divine cosmos watching ourselves. We can identify who we are and witness our truth.

Sexually celibate men and women create a similar experience when they transmute their sexual energy by merging it with divine energy. Obviously, it is more of a transpersonal and psychic experience than if they were orgasmic with a physical lover. Their eyes may or may not be physically open, but their eyes are definitely psychically open. Their eyes are the focal point in front of their love and devotion to the cosmic Mystery.

For Your Consideration: Do you prefer to have the lights on when sexually intimate? Why or why not?

Do you enjoy looking at every single inch of your body and your lover's body carefully and adoringly? Can you bathe your lover's body and enjoy carefully studying his or her body?

What is your relationship with the divine? Do you and your partner pray together? Why or why not? Can you talk to your deities while looking each other in the eyes? Why or why not?

When expressing sexually with your beloved, do you look into his or her eyes and thank your deity aloud for your blessings, your love and devotion, your beloved? Are you willing to do the same during intercourse? Why or why not?

Have you looked into her or his orgasmic eyes?

In the story I am about to share with you, I first witnessed my beloved partner's orgasmic energy in his eyes because we felt the strong desire to freely express appreciation for each other, to claim and honor the goodness and possibilities of our lives, and to celebrate the union of our love. The story of my sexuality is sacred, as is yours, and you and I have the right and responsibility to choose how we share our sacred, appropriate stories—they are not shameful secrets! We simply are selective in how and with whom we share them. When people continually keep their sexual desires secret—confusion and illusion of the sexual dark ages—they are sneaky and silent about their needs. Nevertheless, the common ground of all human beings—from the first to the last breath of life—is the desire for peace, love, pleasure, and ecstatic union with all life. Sexual expression is simply the great metaphor for the desire to live life to the fullest. As humans become more conscious about the divine truth of their sexual energy and its natural gifts, the confusing and shame-based secrets about sexual desire will cease to exist. We will no longer be embarrassed and shy to talk about what is real, and we will know the difference between sacred or secret. Without the presence of shame, we will be able to look into the eyes of all we meet, silently acknowledge our oneness, and send prayers asking for their blessings of a deep union with pleasure, love, and life.

> *Last night was the first time I have ever seen his orgasmic eyes. How could I have missed it? Silly me, sweet silly me!*
>
> *I never imagined I was missing something vitally important in my beloved partner, the amazing man who I love beyond description. Such joy in receiving his passionate, masculine body. I feel so safe in his presence, wrapped inside his tender fierceness, my protective warrior. My Lord, thank you for this brave, kind*

man who offers everything he can possibly give to my body, my love, my safety, my life.

My Lady, you know I love feeling him over me, under me, around me, in me, filling me up with his strength, his power in the world, offering me more than I could ever imagine. Yes, you and my Lord are also in me, over me, under me, and around me offering me every breath I take, even my eternal breath! But, my Lady, he has become my body! Thank you for teaching me how to receive him and for being with me when I do. You are my beauty. You are my tenderness. You are my willingness to be safely cracked open with his focused life. Such synergy! The miracle of sacred synergy, my Lady! Thank you, my Lord and my Lady for this man I love.

His smile, his controlled, adoring smile—I love the way it gives me fair warning of the impending tidal wave, his passionate drive to confidently mold my willing little body. I thought there was not an inch of his body I didn't know and love. Last night, I saw a new place, my Lord. I saw you and my Lady, too. I know you have always witnessed us, but last night, we glimpsed you.

His orgasmic eyes! I didn't recognize his orgasmic eyes! They were not the eyes I knew. His wildly penetrating energy-eyes opened a door for me. When we instantly flew through the door, I was no longer only human. I came face to face with life itself—your cosmic love. It stared me down shouting, "Look at what you can be! Look at who you are! You are more than you ever imagined!"

And so I am looking. Thank you, my Lord and my Lady.

—An Excerpt from the Author's Journal

For Your Consideration: Now in your heart and mind, replace my sacred story with your sacred story. Will you believe that you are more than you ever imagined? Will you believe in your ecstasy? Use your tools for transformation and record your experience in your journal.

There are many ways to be transformed through the energy of our eyes. Sexual intercourse is only one way. You will relate differently to each enlightened expression depending on your age, physical abilities, sexual orientation, gender consciousness, physical health, and many other personal circumstances. You are a sexual being from the moment of your first breath of life until your last breath. Every age and stage of your life offers, or perhaps demands, that you relate to specific enlightened expressions.

Though sexual intercourse can be exquisitely pleasurable, it can be even more powerfully transforming as a metaphor for the masculine and feminine flow of energies—initiating, opening, releasing, and receiving. If you have never or can no longer experience sexual intercourse, be careful to not let the memory or lack of memory create profound frustration, longing, or shame. Physical sexual intercourse and orgasm are just two of the many experiences of the sexually enlightened! If you are a person who has never experienced sexual intercourse or orgasm, or who has been sexually celibate for years or decades, you have the opportunity to become as equally conscious and transformed as any sexually active man or woman.

On the other hand, if you are sexually expressive at this time in your life, learn to look at your partner ninety percent of the time when making love. Turn on the lights and open your eyes. Look at and watch every single part of your partner's body. Look at your own body. Watching your sexual partner with adoration is practice for watching life with adoration. The sixth enlightened expression teaches you to consciously watch all beings that bring deep meaning into your life. Take the time to allow your feminine energy to receive them with adoration. Doing so will reconnect your masculine energy to the deepest, most sacred meaning in your life.

For Your Consideration: Are you comfortable looking into the eyes of people you know? What about people you don't know? Why or why not?

Do you take the time to enjoy watching nature? Do you know how to look into the eyes of all beings? Is it possible that nature is watching and loving you through its energy eyes as much as you watch and love nature through your energy eyes? Do you practice embracing and honoring the common ground of all beings?

This book creates a mirror for you. What do you see about your sexuality in the mirror? What don't you want to see?

If you can't see the cosmos through your human eyes, it is possible to see it through your energy eyes. Is it possible to explore the energy of the cosmos through your lover's eyes?

✿

Who is your God? Does your God watch you? How do you watch your God? Is your God's sexual energy you? Who are you?

Remember, sexual enlightenment—erotic pleasure, love, and union with the divine cosmos—is a metaphor for life's greatest and eternal gifts, and certainly your inner and outer eyes help you search for and find those gifts. Furthermore, is it possible that all of Earth's beings are searching for the same gifts through their inner and outer eyes? Is it possible that you could see your deity in the eyes of all beings? Allow yourself to be humble, open-minded, and teachable. Acknowledge fear, release it, and open up to love. Allow the astonishing journey to sexual enlightenment to be more than you ever imagined. Witness your miracles.

In this following story of my friendship with Queen, time and space will not allow for detailed descriptions of the deep and various meanings she held for my family, friends, and me. Frankly, many who knew her thought of her as an angel, not only because of her behavior, but also because of a sense of her as a spiritual messenger and protector. Humans in her presence were often transformed into a calm, loving, and unusually aware state. For 16 years, she expressed her love, devotion, and sensitivity through her physical form of a beautiful dog, a Black Labrador.

Though I adored everything about her, there was something special about the way she communicated with me through her eyes. Countless times, she silently called to me through her thoughts, interrupting my various forms of preoccupation and entrancement.

Upon hearing her thoughts, I felt compelled to disengage from a book, conversation, sleep, meditation, or deep emotion to find her looking at me. She was motionless, yet through an indescribable and often haunting stare, her eyes were intensely acknowledging and confirming our communication.

Though she was calm by nature, the last year of her life the pace slowed down considerably. While slowly strolling in the woods near our cabin in the Canadian Rocky Mountains, I would often burst into laughter as I watched her, that wondrous source of pure delight as she mimicked the slightly swayed-back and slowly swinging hindquarters of a confident, lazily strolling lioness.

Our morning ritual was always the same. It involved my opening the back door of our cabin for her, the familiar swinging-swaying meandering as she peacefully headed through the door toward the elegant forest, and then halfway to her destination, the momentary but mysterious, slow turn of her head as she calmly fired that familiar laser-look from her eyes, once again allowing us to acknowledge our unquestionable devotion. It was our tender yet hauntingly powerful secret ritual.

However, there was another less apparent yet more encompassing response in her eyes, the energy of the connection that for a moment could carry me to a transpersonal realm, a place in my consciousness incapable of being described with words. It was a form of communication that I could never identify, and only after her death did I finally find a way to claim its meaning.

Her death was a surprise to me. Though I knew that she wouldn't live in her body forever, I couldn't quite imagine life without her. So, I suppose I did not consciously prepare for her death as carefully as I might have had I faced my truth. Her truth came on a day when I had just finished an event that Queen always anticipated and attended—my teaching piano to people young and old. It was as though Queen waited until the last student left the village before she began her transition.

When the sacred time began, her labored breathing claimed my attention. As our eyes met in communion for the last time, I could see her life force quickly beginning to dissipate. I knew she was dying. "No, God, no," I panicked.

Simultaneously through my weeping and smiling, I begged her not to leave me and reassured her that it was safe to go. Within 15 minutes, the physical life of my dear friend had come to an end. My heart was silent and broken. I couldn't breathe.

During the days that followed, part of my grieving process involved trying to understand what happened between us when our eyes met. The origin of the forceful energy was a mystery to me, and the need to understand it grew stronger daily. Somehow, instinctively I knew following the strange energy to its source would lead me not only to Queen but also to the source of our love and devotion. Therefore, I wanted to bathe in it.

A few days later, the answer was given to me. It happened during the sacred time of night when all worlds become one—the birthplace of dreams, visions, and mystical journeys. I rested in my bed, knowing that she was no longer sleeping

beside it; the hollow, sick hole in my gut would not let me for-
get. I cried out to Queen and the Mystery, pleading to know
the answer to my question. "What was the feeling in our eyes?
Queen, Queen, what was it? What was it?"

What I felt and heard next was overwhelming. Thoughts
and feelings rang in my brainheart, dissolving awareness of my
body and allowing me to fully receive the following communi-
cation, "It was me, darling, it was me. The look in Queen's eyes
was me. She is my daughter, as are you. It was me speaking to
you through Queen. Feel me. Know that I am with you. Know
that you are not alone. Know that we are one."

I knew immediately who was communing with me: it was
Earth, the thought of whom swells my heart and brings tears of
adoration, thankfulness, and devotion. All of those times that
I felt the mysterious energy from Queen's eyes, its source was
Earth—the grand being who had eventually introduced me to
my Lady, my Divine Mother.

Suddenly, intense ideas and feelings forced themselves into
my awareness and for a few minutes demanded recognition and
embodiment. As quickly as the words were received from Earth,
I scrambled to scratch them on paper:

"Tell my noble wounded warriors who have fought to
protect themselves and others that the struggle is over and that
they can come home to me and rest. The war is over. Tell them
that I live and speak through the silence in their hearts.

The plants and animals send thoughts to you through your
love for them. Love is the vehicle. Love and oneness. Someday
the whole world will hear them speak. For now, they can speak
to you and others who will listen. Continue to believe in your
distant drum.

Daughters and sons listen to your hearts and heal. Search for the words that are missing, words that help all to remember that humans have forgotten who they are.

It is time for a sacred marriage of Heaven and Earth. Allow the Light to shine by believing in the divinity of this physical plane. Your role is to teach your sisters and brothers that I am alive and I listen and speak.

Listen to your heart, my little one. It is your destiny to believe, Brave One Who Holds the Light. It is your lesson to have the courage to speak and write about your personal vision, about what you witness so passionately."

—An Excerpt from the Author's Journal

This personal story I share with you was timely and pivotal in my life. I was shaken by the experience and didn't share it with anyone for many years, but I never forgot it—a new course was quietly but irrevocably set for me. Yes, the unique story is my story, and everyone has a unique story! Our stories are often hard to share because the message sets us apart from the rest of the world—it clarifies our specialness. Perhaps we think if we share our stories, we will become more visible and that might be frightening. Therefore, to be able to stand joyfully naked before the world, we first learn to acknowledge our fear, release it, and open up to self-love. Two of the nine natural gifts of sexual energy are to be responsible for personal choices and to transform Earth. Your unique life's purpose and the two natural gifts are linked together. Personal clarity and vision is created through sexual enlightenment.

For Your Consideration: What can your eyes teach you? What closed doors in your personal life would you like your eyes to open? Will you embrace revisions? Use your tools for shifting insights. Create a ritual to celebrate your new vision.

If you believe your deity creates and lives in all life, will you open your eyes wide to see all life? Would your God want you to practice seeing the gifts? What gifts do you give to the world? What is your life's purpose?

Will you allow your orgasmic energy to lead you to your God? When your sexual energy is flowing, are you willing to open your orgasmic eyes and witness miracles?

Do you understand how much human beings suffer because of sexual ignorance and violence? Do you or does anyone you know suffer? What is your wildest revision of humankind's sexual consciousness? Will you help create it?

Your journey into healthy sexuality is important for the world. Together, all human beings will create the evolutionary process of sexual enlightenment. Your creative insights and personal commitment to sexual transformation are essential for the human race to awaken. Will you let the world see the orgasmic truth in your eyes?

ᴥ 14 ᴧ

Seventh Enlightened Expression —
Unite Sexual Energy with the Divine

*T*he seventh enlightened expression of sexual energy is symbolized by the top or crown of the head. Tipping the head backward or forward is a universal gesture of reverence. The seventh enlightened expression symbolizes the revered knowledge that divine energy and sexual energy are the same. We become conscious of this truth by relating to the divine when our sexual energy is flowing. As we learn to experience the union of divine and sexual energy, we forever transform our relationships with all beings.

Ideally, when we are very young, we are taught about spirituality in simple and sweet concepts that our innocence will understand. It is the beginning of a gathering of information that will last a lifetime. When we are very young, we are also taught about the spiritual source of our life force and the pleasant ways we can feel it in the entire body. We are taught these things in tender and safe concepts that our innocence will understand. It is also the beginning of the gathering of information that will last a lifetime. These concepts about sexuality prepare us for sexual health.

Ideally, as we grow through puberty, a more specific understanding of sexuality occurs as we learn through self-pleasuring, prayer, and meditation to consciously and simultaneously feel sexual energy and the love of the divine. In this context, it is a spiritual tool similar to fasting, chanting, dancing, meditating, singing, reading sacred text, and so forth.

We acknowledge the intention to invite God into the heart, mind, and body in order to be spiritually guided and loved while we are cloaked in the clarity of this mystical sexual expression. In doing so, we change or transmute sexual energy, and we no longer perceive it as being separate from divine energy! We feel a union with the Divine Masculine and the Divine Feminine.

Once a person learns to equate sexual energy with his or her unique essence and the spirit that flows in and around it through the tender practice of self-pleasuring combined with prayer and meditation, he or she may be ready to do the same with another person. Then, beloved partners gradually and carefully learn this spiritual practice together. Their sexual consciousness is greatly expanded as they open up to their love for the divine. Eventually, their sexual union includes prayer and meditation.

This powerful sexual and spiritual experience is the result of a commitment on the part of celibate men and women or committed lovers to learn to explore the spiritual nature of sexuality, to be humble, open-minded, and teachable. There is absolutely no guilt or shame present; it has been released from the prison of the human body. Through erotic love and passionate reverence, a person is making the profound statement: "My God, I come to Thee."

Why would a person want to practice this kind of sexual expression? "Why not simply pray?" you might ask.

"That is certainly good," I would say.

"Why not simply self-pleasure?" you might ask.

"That is certainly an option," I would say.

"But, why put the two together?" you might ask.

"So you feel wholeness, holiness, and oneness!" I would say.

Sexual enlightenment creates the consciousness that your pure energies are whole, not broken and fragmented. Feeling sexual energy in the genitals is the most direct way to feel your unique energy core, the home of the divine. Sexual energy is the door that opens you to the freedom and love of your pure cosmic energy core. Therefore, you acknowledge that sexual energy and divine energy are not separate. In acknowledging the union, you protect yourself from the confusing and distorted beliefs about sexuality that destroy love and life—fear, shame, sexual repression, sexual obsession, sexual addiction, and sexual violence. By releasing yourself from negative and destructive sexual beliefs and experiences, you can find peace and eternal love. You courageously and lovingly face and release shame, the Great Illusion, and you exit the dark ages.

For Your Consideration: When you feel sexual energy, you are feeling your God's energy. You can claim your powerful inheritance and live with peace and passion, or you can reject it and live with shame and confusion. You have the choice. What do you want to do?

✣❦✣

*You now have the information and opportunity to create
sexual health and brilliance so you can properly and wisely
counsel and teach children and teenagers about the truth of
sexual energy. What do you want to do?*

❧ ─────────────────────────────────── ☙

You now have the opportunity to learn how to become conscious
of the union of primal sexual energy and divine energy. Learning
and practicing the following technique is one of the most important
things you will ever do.

FIFTH SPIRITUAL TOOL — MERGE
SEXUAL ENERGY WITH DIVINE ENERGY

Consciously merging primal sexual energy with divine energy
provides a powerful path to health and peace. This applies to all
people, regardless of why they are seeking enlightenment. I have had
the privilege of seeing many clients make great strides in accomplishing their individual goals because they learned to transmute
sexual energy and commune with the divine. Of these individuals,
many felt an intense desire to change the world for the better and,
therefore, wanted to explore personal empowerment. Some clients
who were clergy members felt their knowledge and counseling about
sexuality were inadequate so they wanted to be enlightened about
spiritual and sexual energies. Some prosperous individuals wanted
to begin the astounding journey to sexual enlightenment and use
their financial resources to spread the work to others around the

world. In contrast, some clients were ending marriages or relationships and seeking spiritual inspiration to understand what went wrong and how they should prepare to successfully choose a new life and partner. Additionally, clients who were struggling with addictions to sexually obsessive behaviors such as prostitution and pornography were urgently searching for a way out of the darkness so they could save their relationships and lead productive lives. But no matter how different their individual goals were, this powerful technique became a life-changing step on their journey to sexual enlightenment.

Before you practice transmuting neutral sexual energy by consciously reuniting it with divine energy, make sure you have practiced identifying and releasing any shame that may be living in your energy body. If you haven't released shame, you are not ready for this technique.

When unreleased shame dwells within, you may feel very uneasy about transmuting sexual energy into divine energy. Addressing and releasing shame is a tricky part of sexual growth and healing. I wish I could personally guide every person through this experience, but remember, you have the best guide possible— the One who created you. Always ask for divine guidance and protection during your journey into the new realm of sexual reality.

Sexual enlightenment is a powerful, healthy, shame-free, and enlivened state of consciousness based on a deliberate, focused relationship with divinely created energy. By relating to the source, nature, and nine natural gifts of sexual energy, you can consciously unite with the miraculous energy that is in you and throughout the cosmos. Because your relationship with your sexuality is a metaphor for your relationship with life, you will be exploring great mysteries of life.

To successfully enter the gates of expanded consciousness and transform your limiting beliefs and actions requires a willingness to be open to change. Remember to embrace as fully as possible the following traits and qualities: Be present and conscious in the moment. Have faith in the goodness and possibilities of life. Acknowledge and release fear, and open up to love. Embrace and honor the common ground of all beings. Believe in your ecstasy. Freely express appreciation. Witness and acknowledge daily miracles. Be humble, open-minded, and teachable.

 STEP ONE: Create a sacred space. Candles, gentle music, oils, and bathing can help create reverence. Prayer and meditation help to affirm your intentions. Use your tools for shifting insights. Gently touch and stimulate your whole body or have your partner gently touch you for as long as you need.

Practice the Breath of Life technique. Ideally, you will be very familiar with this breathing technique before you use it to merge sexual energy with love for and of the divine. A brief review follows.

A. Position yourself so your back is straight and your shoulders are relaxed. Direct your mind to your pelvic floor and the warmth of the Earth flowing into you. Close your mouth and inhale, pulling Earth's energy up through your energy core all the way to the crown of your head and out to the cosmos. Visualize the energy instantly flowing up through your core from the bottom to the top. Feel the slight tension and sound of your breath in your nostrils, but not in your throat. Relax your entire body.

B. While holding your breath contract and expand two times the muscles that help you stop urinating.

C. Direct your mind to the crown of your head and the divine energy from the cosmos flowing into you. Open your mouth and exhale, guiding the energy down through your energy core all the way to the pelvic floor and into the Earth. Relax your entire body.

Repeat the Breath of Life several times.

⚬ STEP TWO: Practice merging neutral sexual energy with love energy, which is described fully in Chapter 10. Ideally, you will already be very familiar with this process. A brief review follows:

A. Fill your heart with as much love as you can by simply giving yourself the opportunity to be quiet, calm, open, and receptive. Finish this step by taking several deep, full breaths.

B. Lovingly touch your whole body or have your partner gently touch you. Create sexual energy by gently stimulating your genitals. Discontinue the touching and breathe deeply and fully.

C. Gently merge love energy and sexual energy. Rest while breathing fully and deeply.

⚬ STEP THREE: Take the opportunity to commune with the divine in your personal, unique way. Claim your intention to become sexually enlightened by living from a clear, healthy, and sacred energy core. Use the Breath of Life technique to help you feel your energy core.

⚬ STEP FOUR: Gently and slowly begin to self-pleasure. If you have a partner, ask him or her to observe you as opposed to pleasuring you during this intensely delicate and personal activity.

⚬ STEP FIVE: Feel your spiritual communication while also feeling your sexual energy. Continue this process as long as you feel good about it. Remember, your sexual energy level should be low. (Learning to increase sexual energy while experiencing spiritual energy takes practice and concentration.)

Stop if you become aware of any shame developing in your energy body. Acknowledge and release these energetic thought forms by using the shame releasing spiritual tool described in detail in Chapter 4: Shame—The Great Illusion.

✿ STEP SIX: Relax and gently breathe for several minutes.

Once you have practiced this spiritual tool by self-pleasuring, have your partner help you with the process as you practice communicating about your needs. This is a spiritual practice that uses touch, words and sounds, the eyes, and your healthy breathing to communicate. Expect it to be a very different experience from normal self-pleasuring that usually reinforces the illusion of the separation of spiritual and sexual energies. When both of you know how to consciously relate to the union of energies separately, you are ready to slowly integrate this spiritual practice into your physical and sexual expressions together.

Please remember that while masturbation and transmutation both involve the use of sexual energy, they are profoundly different and shouldn't be confused. Masturbation—a sexual experience resulting from the use of impersonal, primal sexual energy—can be a highly pleasurable experience. It is also a form of spiritually unprotected sex that can lead to serious problems because it reinforces the consciousness of separateness.

On the other hand, transmutation—a spiritual tool—reinforces the consciousness of wholeness. This spiritual experience is created by merging primal sexual energy with divine energy by self-pleasuring and praying or meditating. The highly pleasurable experience that can lead to spiritual ecstasy, inspiration, and personal revelation is spiritually protected sex because of the conscious relationship with deity.

⸎ 15 ⸎

EIGHTH ENLIGHTENED EXPRESSION —
RECEIVE INSPIRATION
AND REVELATION

*T*he eighth enlightened expression of sexual energy is symbolized by a circle, which represents the core of energy that pulses throughout the center of our bodies. We think of the energy core as a divine river of life, our exclusive home. Ideally, we diligently strive to keep our centers pure and clear. We learn to go home to our centers through various means such as prayer, meditation, nature, love, beauty, and music so we may be inspired and guided by the divine.

We also learn to connect to our divine centers through sexual energy. After we learn how to consciously reunite sexual energy with love energy, we learn to relate to the union of sexual energy and divine energy through self-pleasuring and praying or meditating. When we are ready, we also learn to relate to the union of sexual energy and divine energy through sexual expression with our intimate partner and prayer or meditation.

When celibate men and women or intimate partners have consciously and purposely learned to use all eight enlightened expressions of sexual energy, they may well discover they have become so creative in their sexual expressions that they are creating a new path with every step they take on their journey—a journey that is astoundingly personal! They know there is no tool more powerful for healing the destructive results of improper use of sexual energy than the positive and creative use of divine life force. Not only are they consciously using the divine sexual energy to enliven and heal their bodies, minds, and spirits, they are also asking for and receiving inspiration, guidance, and revelation regarding their deepest dreams, lives, relationships, families, and communities, and all of Earth's beings.

The transmutation of sexual energy into divine love and will within our energy bodies is a tool for the evolution of human consciousness—the creative power of which is beyond comprehension. We are ready for it now.

Imagine what would happen to the human race if each person's profoundly unique gifts to the world were discovered and consciously developed and nurtured without fear and limitation. Then, what would happen if we used our expanded minds and hearts to identify the highest good for human beings, for all Earth's beings? How would the structure of government and business change worldwide? What new goals for world health and peace would we obtain through the use of science and technology? Geniuses of the heart and mind would be common, so how might they use art, music, literature, film, and other forms of communication to inspire and free the world of shame and destruction? And perhaps the most exciting question of all—how would all future generations of human beings live because their ancestors came out of the dark ages of sexuality? Consciously changing and responsibly guiding the divine energy within—sexual enlightenment—is the next phase of human evolution, and it is possible for you, for the whole world. You can help create it.

—————————————————————————

For Your Consideration: Will you learn to transmute your divinely created sexual energy to help you learn who you are, why you are here, and where you are going?

What do you want to create with your partner—the Master of Creation? Think and feel deeply as you communicate your truth. Know that your partnership with your deity will make it happen. Watch it happen as you use the spiritual tool of divinely created sexual energy.

Will you become a shame-free and sexually enlightened adult who will inspire and teach others, especially children and teenagers?

—————————————————————————

THE CIRCLE OF ENLIGHTENED EXPRESSIONS OF SEXUAL ENERGY

The eight enlightened expressions of sexual energy create a state of expanded consciousness that releases blocked energy in your body so that you learn to co-create with God. One by one the eight enlightened expressions lift the veil to reveal the truth that will change your life—and this truth is more than you ever imagined.

I have presented the enlightened expressions starting at the lowest part of the body and ending at the highest point of the body in what would appear to form a vertical line. However, it is better to think of the enlightened expressions as forming a circle so you won't be misled into thinking one is more important than the other. All eight expressions hold equal importance and are interconnected. For example, if placed on a vertical line, the first enlightened expression (Earth) may appear less important than the seventh enlightened expression (spirit). Both expressions involve awareness of sexual energy and spiritual energy. In the circle of enlightened expressions, the first and seventh expressions are connected by the eighth expression (receive inspiration, guidance, and revelation from the divine). Therefore, the three expressions can be operating in unison—the inspiration and guidance and love of the divine cosmic universe (eighth enlightened expression) is felt and known in the body (first enlightened expression) and spirit (seventh enlightened expression).

The astounding experience of childbirth is a powerful way to explain how the first, seventh, and eighth enlightened expressions operate in unison. Imagine a woman giving birth. The primal life force in the brave woman is naturally opening her body, even without the help of her conscious mind. Ideally, her body is in the process of giving birth to the creative results between herself and her beloved intimate partner. The body of their baby is emerging from the miraculous union of the spiritual body (seventh enlightened expression) and the physical body (first enlightened expression). This pure and innocent spirit may have just been held and counseled by the creator—the Divine Masculine and Divine Feminine (eighth enlightened expression). Perhaps the last place the Divine touched the tiny newborn child before he or she entered the Earth was on the top of the head (seventh enlightened expression).

The mystery of life is certainly apparent when a child is miraculously born. The mystical union of body and spirit is beyond comprehension. The journey is graciously creative and potentially destructive; just like birth and death, just like sexuality.

A wonderful technique that bathes your energy body with your sexual energy is presented below.

Sixth Spiritual Tool — Full Body Expanded Pleasure

The purpose of this spiritual practice is to empower you to bathe your energy core and energy body with sexual energy. This spiritual tool can transport sexual energy from the genitals throughout the entire body, resulting in great pleasure. This spiritual tool can also be used to direct sexual energy into specific places in the body to promote health. Whether you practice this technique alone or with a partner, it can help you to consciously feel divine energy in the entire body and create a very strong orgasmic energy.[1]

Consciously filling the body with sexual energy is an essential breathing technique for anyone who wants to achieve sexual enlightenment. Many of my clients have found this technique easy to master and used it to move themselves closer to achieving their goals—though their objectives varied immensely. For instance, while the goal of some clients was to become the best lover possible, others were concerned about erectile dysfunction and premature ejaculation and wanted to learn how to move sexual energy from the genitals to the upper body to expand their pleasure and prolong lovemaking. Some healthcare professionals were seeking insights that would enable them to successfully help patients struggling with physical issues of sexuality. While clients who were physically unable to express themselves sexually due to injuries and diseases yearned to understand and experience breathing and energy techniques that would offer them pleasurable alternatives.

Before you can learn how to bathe the entire body in sexual energy—full body expanded pleasure—you will need to familiarize yourself with and become proficient at using the following spiritual tools: Breath of Life (Chapter 5), Merge Sexual Energy with Love Energy (Chapter 10), and Merge Sexual Energy with Divine Energy (Chapter 14). In addition, you should be skilled at identifying and releasing shame from your energy body (Chapter 4). If you have practiced all four of these techniques, learning to bathe the entire body with sexual energy will be easy!

Before you begin, create a sacred space. Candles, gentle music, oils, and bathing can help create reverence. In addition, prayer and meditation affirm your honorable intentions. For as long as you need, gently touch and stimulate your whole body or have your partner gently touch you.

✆ STEP ONE: Create a low intensity of sexual energy. Be aware of its divine source.

✆ STEP TWO: Stop stimulating the genitals. Take two deep breaths using the Breath of Life. (Remember to take your consciousness to the pelvic floor before you inhale.) As you breathe, use your mental intentions to guide the energy you are receiving in the pelvic floor from Earth up through your energy core. The sexual energy you are feeling in your genitals will follow.

✒ STEP THREE: Be aware of sexual energy beginning to move out of your genitals and up into your belly. You may feel a tingling sensation, warmth, or sexual energy, but as you continue to practice these three steps, you will feel more direct sexual energy.

✒ STEP FOUR: Slowly and consciously repeat steps 1–3. Increase your sexual energy to a moderate level. If you are breathing correctly, you will feel sexual energy coming out of your genitals and up into your chest. Eventually, you should be able to feel sexual energy in your throat and head. Remember the divine source of the energy.

Obviously, you will decide when to stop practicing this powerful tool, but if you continue raising your sexual energy and repeating the steps, you should be able to feel sexual energy throughout the entire body. Men may lose some of the firmness of their erections when they properly use the breathing technique; however, the firmness will return as soon as the genitals are stimulated again.

Regardless of sexual preference, partners and singles who practice spiritual sexuality can learn to integrate this remarkable spiritual tool into all eight enlightened expressions for creating sexual enlightenment! For example, when your sexual expression is focused only on the first enlightened expression, using this spiritual tool will help you feel the intense, driving, primal energy of lust throughout the body, creating marvelous, erotic experiences.

Integrating the technique into all eight enlightened expressions takes practice and dedication. Improvise, be creative, and make changes depending on what works best for you. Doing so is a personal and astoundingly intimate process that takes time. But, what a wonderful way to spend time.

For Your Consideration: What are your deepest dreams for your life, your relationships and family, for the world and Earth? What kind of a plan will you make? Will you trust and use the resources inside you? Will you harness the creative power of your sacred energies to co-create with the divine and, therefore, realize your goals and dreams?

The history of my journey to nature, sexuality, and spirituality is preserved through decades of my journal writings. In reviewing all of them, I found that though the same themes repeated over and over in a multitude of settings—hot red sand or cool white sheets; erotic, primal sex or divine union; intense celibate explorer or beloved sexual partner—the constantly personal results were the same—guidance inspiration, revelation, and transformation.

My explorations and adventures taught me who I am and why I am here so I could trust who I was becoming. I couldn't have found myself without personal guidance, inspiration, and revelation from Earth, my Lady, and my Lord. The transformation occurred by using the spiritual tool of combining my sexual energy with prayer and meditation described in this book.

As the sun rises, so will you. Speak in Our name. We are one. Our children need to hear what you need to say. You will be guided. We will speak to you. We will speak to you and We will speak through you. You will be filled with strength and courage.

Everything you need will be given to you. Everything is in perfect timing. We will show you the way and take your hand because we hear you asking. We feel your deep love for us and know that you are hungry to help. As you see beauty, feel your own. Honor your rhythm, which is very slow and peaceful. As you love Us, love yourself so We may speak through you.

Believe and go forth with your work. Do not be afraid to speak your truth. Do not be afraid to say what you do. Do not be afraid to say what you know. Speak your truth and the world will listen.

—An Excerpt from the Author's Journal

My revealed life's purpose described above is uniquely mine. I have learned throughout the years to humbly honor and believe in it without a doubt. During my work in private sessions and workshops, I have had the tender privilege of listening to thousands of people share their unique life's purpose. My prayer for you is that you know what your life's purpose is and believe in it without a doubt. I wish I could listen to you share it—that we could stand beside each other and acknowledge our oneness and equality in this grand divine cosmos!

For Your Consideration: To live as deeply and fully as possible—directed and focused on your life's purpose—are there questions you need to have answered? Do you need directions clarified? How do you want to be encouraged and supported?

Do you believe in a personal or impersonal deity? Do you
believe in personal guidance and revelation from your deity?
If so, how are you inspired and guided? Are you willing to use
the astonishingly powerful tool of transmuting sexual energy
to see your brilliance and genius, and are you willing to give
it to the world?

༄

Will you join fellow human beings worldwide who will
be known to future generations as the brave pioneers who
created the dawn of sexual enlightenment and changed the
world forever?

Notes: Chapter 15—Eighth Enlightened Expression—Receive Inspiration and Revelation

[1]Muir & Muir, *Conscious Loving*. 1989.

Sexuality
A DECLARATION
to the World

We human beings of this great planet, Earth, solemnly declare we have the inherent spiritual right and responsibility to understand who we are, why we are here, and where we are going. Therefore, we have the inherent right and responsibility to be sexually enlightened. Our sexual energy is not separate from our spiritual energy. The inseparable union is the divinely created life energy that flows through us. The highly pleasurable sensations we feel in our genitals is a direct experience of that powerful force. By relating to the divine source, nature, and natural gifts of our sexual energy we consciously unite with astounding cosmic energy of which we are part. We become greatly empowered as we use the gift to create great peace and goodness in the world. Therefore, we acknowledge the following:

The *Ideal Chronology* of
✍ NINE NATURAL GIFTS ✍
of *Sexual Energy*

✍ *First Natural Gift* ✍
Relate Generally to Divinely Created Energy

The energy of Earth's sensuous and creative nature helps us honor the energy of our own sensuous and creative nature. To relate naturally to energy in the world, we learn as young children that the energy of life flowing through Earth also flows through us.

Though we are too young to be presented with the adult concept of sexual energy and sexual expression, we certainly relate to the sensuous Earth around us. We are given experiences in nature that will ground us safely and fully in our own physical bodies as we are provided with as many opportunities possible to experience the pleasure, joy, and beauty of the Earth and the human body. The experiences teach us how to feel and relate to divinely created energy present everywhere in the cosmos.

Becoming sexually enlightened adults is directly related to our love of Earth's energy we learn to feel as children. Therefore, we are given opportunities to love and honor our bodies and Earth as vehicles for living and loving life. As we continue to live our lives, further teachings and practices related to energy are presented to us and learned in appropriate ways, depending on our age, level of understanding, and emotional maturity. Consequently, when we eventually mature into adulthood, the human body, in harmony with the Earth's body constitutes the beloved schoolroom of high, conscious learning about sexual energy and sexual expressions.

✒ Second Natural Gift ✑
Relate Directly to Divinely Created Energy

Because we have learned to feel energy all around us, we as young children are ready to learn simple concepts about energy. Educated adults help us to realize that we have a physical body and an energy body, as well as the simple idea that an energy core or river runs up and down our bodies. We are wisely taught to breathe well because it is a very healthy, fun practice and it also helps us understand, visualize, and feel energy in our bodies.

When appropriate, we acknowledge the pleasurable feelings in our genitals and that the feelings are the direct experiences with the life force flowing in the energy core. Our parents understand well that we naturally feel sexual energy in the body and genitals, for example, as a result of riding a bike, swinging in a swing, taking a bath, feeling the warmth of urine, or the glow of the sun. Because our bodies are a source of pleasure, it is also natural and healthy for us to explore the feelings of being alive in our own bodies.

As shame-free adults, we are prepared for the important opportunity of offering our children positive responses to their exploration of their precious and fragile sense of selves. Being wise adults, we understand and accept children's interests in the world of possibilities and allow them the innocent experience of feeling pleasure without inflicting destructive shame. When a child obviously feels pleasure and excitement because of experiences in the environment, or when a child casually touches his or her own body and genitals with obvious pleasure and curiosity—it is a perfect time to learn that what he or she is feeling is the divine gift of life felt everywhere on Earth. We teach children this miraculous force is also in them as easily as we acknowledge their interest in the beauty of a flower, the antics of a silly pet, or the mystery of the heavenly moon.

As children, we learn this fact about energy so that when we become teenagers and have more intense experiences with our life force in the genitals, we are not confused or overwhelmed; it is simply the next step in our lives. Our sexual energy will be understood and respected. Puberty is the ideal time for us to be exposed to the divine source, nature, and nine sacred natural gifts of sexual energy.

Because we are very familiar with breathing properly, we are able to easily understand about free flowing or trapped energy within us, and as teenagers we are wisely taught by educated adults about the trapped energy in the body and the illusion we call destructive shame as well as techniques for identifying and liberating the imprisoned energy. We are greatly empowered as we learn the differences between constructive and destructive forms of guilt and shame.

As adults, we are committed to protecting our children and teenagers from inappropriate or harmful experiences with touch they might receive by anyone in their environment. However, if a child or teenager has been exposed to inappropriate sexual experiences, they may exhibit more than a casual interest in the body, sexual energy, and their genitals. Moreover, we understand their unnatural behavior, protect them and get them help.

◦Third Natural Gift◦
Consciously Unite Primal Sexual Energy with Divine Energy

When appropriate and as soon as interested, as teenagers, we learn the technique for merging neutral life force—the sexual energy we feel in our genitals—with love energy. We practice this spiritual tool while self-pleasuring and meditating or praying. Next, while self-pleasuring and praying or meditating, we learn the spiritual technique for merging our primal sexual energy with divine energy—the two are wed and protect each other.

This spiritual tool for consciously changing or transmuting our primal sexual energy to spiritual energy is best learned before we begin to enter committed relationships and marriage—before our sexual energy becomes exclusively related to our partners or spouses. We know we are only dependent on the divine for sexual expression. We are taught that when we are mature adults, this kind of sexual experience can eventually become a very personal, powerful form of communion and prayer with a beloved, committed partner and the divine—the glue of our relationships.

✐ Fourth Natural Gift ✑
Be Responsible for Choices

The sexual feelings and drives of our physical bodies are a result of our direct experiences with energy in our energy bodies. Furthermore, these powerful sexual feelings demand we explore and become responsible for personal choices pertaining to how we use the powerful energy. Therefore, sexual feelings call to us in powerfully direct manners. They say: "Hello! God is here! You are alive! Feel your life! Learn to understand and respect your energy in order to transform your life! The gift of power within you can be used to destroy or create life, love, and peace. Which choices will you make?"

Because as teenagers or young adults we have learned to consciously unite our sexual energy with divine love by self-pleasuring and praying and meditating, we are ready to learn about being responsible for making choices about how to use our sexual energy with another person. We learn from shame-free and educated adults about the constructive and destructive consequences of the use of sexual energy. Therefore, we are greatly prepared to face the world of possibilities and make choices that are in alignment with our personal values.

Learning to consciously unite primal sexual energy with divine energy in our energy cores does not diminish our healthy sexual intensity or curiosity. Nevertheless, it does provide a spiritual context for the continued interest in expressing our sexual energy. On the other hand, we are taught we can be celibate for years, decades, or our entire lives and be balanced and healthy as long as we raise sexual energy and relate it to the love of our gods. Consequently, we are protected from sexual obsessions and addictions that might result from the practice of raising impersonal primal sexual energy and combining it with impersonal sexual experiences. We are aware of and protect ourselves from exposure to unconscious, sexually uneducated, manipulative, and seductive expressions of primal sexual energy that are exhibited by teenagers and adults in cultures around the world and the resulting energy of thought forms that can invade the body and create illusions of shame. Just as we would not intentionally create a physical disease, we would not intentionally create an energy disease.

☙ *Fifth Natural Gift* ❧
Honor Gender

Knowing we are divinely created helps us to better understand and accept the unique and natural changes that occur during puberty. Because we have been well educated about divine energy all our lives, as teenagers, we are prepared to honor gender needs and differences. We practice learning about the masculine and feminine energies within and between people, and we relate to the ideal Divine Feminine and Divine Masculine within our energy cores as models for our intense new feelings and thoughts. We are beginning a life-long journey of relating with respect to gender differences.

☙ *Sixth Natural Gift* ❧
Create and Sustain a Pure Energy Core

As young adults, we learn to use divinely created energy as a tool for sustaining a pure energy core—free from the stress and negativity of the human world—because we have fully integrated the first five natural gifts of sexual energy into our lives. Since we can identify and relate to our unique, natural energy essence that flows in the energy core, we under-

stand masculine and feminine energies and we honor gender. We have practiced transmuting our primal sexual energy through self-pleasuring and meditating, and therefore, we are ready to use the energy to create and sustain the pure energy core that flows up and down the body. We know our energy essence is the exclusive home of the *Divine Feminine* and *Divine Masculine* within us and the divine energies provide the astounding inner strength and enlightened consciousness to relate to the human world of possibilities.

✎ Seventh Natural Gift ✑
Enjoy Sexual Pleasure

Gradually and appropriately in expressions that are respectful of the values of ourselves and others, we are ready to explore and be responsible for physical and sexual pleasure.

As young adults, we date others because it is a wonderful way to enjoy life. It is also the way we learn about relationships. We discover what our friends think and how they feel as we learn about their values, dreams, and goals. When we are ready, it is appropriate and healthy for us as young adults to learn about physical intimacy. These activities provide opportunities for us to learn about personal choices because we learn to communicate consciously about touch. We are encouraged by parents and other adults to enjoy being with our peers in appropriate and wholesome ways. These experiences teach us about gender and sexual feelings, and how to be comfortable being honest and emotionally intimate and to enjoy pleasure without compromising our personal boundaries, values, and spiritual goals. Our sexual maturity will be based on this important and honored education. We freely discuss sexuality and spirituality.

Finally, we may be ready for committed relationships and marriages in which we learn to relate our sexual energy to a sacred lover as well as the divine. Becoming fully expressive sexually requires wisdom, education, and practice so we can ensure that our energy cores remain clear—the exclusive home of our Gods. We are not naïve or shame-filled explorers—we are sexually enlightened adults. Consequently, we have been learning to keep all aspects of our lives outside our energy essence, and now we will learn perhaps the most important one—to keep our committed relationships outside our unique cores so that we can maintain spiritual balance and peace regardless of what is happening in the relationship.

This mature skill allows us to receive the divine guidance we need to create successful, committed relationships and marriages. We use the eight enlightened expressions for sexual and spiritual health as tools for transporting and transmuting sexual energy together—a highly advanced spiritual practice. In time, we as sacred lovers who have prepared all our lives for sexual expression with a sacred spouse may well discover that we are so creative in our sexual expressions that we are creating a new path with every step we take on our journeys.

✍ Eighth Natural Gift ✍
Transform the Earth

Through prayer and meditation, we transport and transmute neutral sexual energy to discover, develop, and create our unique talents and gifts—to become natural geniuses. Hence, our personal goals, visions, and creative projects are realized. As sexually educated people, we use divine sexual energy to help heal physical, emotional, mental, and spiritual wounds and illnesses. We understand there is no tool more appropriate or powerful for healing the destructive results of the use of sexual energy than the conscious use of transmuted sexual energy. In our maturity and wisdom, we use the same energy to help heal and transform the world and Earth. We are visionaries and leaders in all fields who change the world by transmuting our sexual energy and using it powerfully and ethically.

✍ Ninth Natural Gift ✍
Procreate

The miraculous, creative force of eternal love that we as committed, married partners feel when we express ourselves sexually helps us receive new life into the world. We create the family unit, and in doing so, co-create with God. Because we began our spiritual and sexual education as children, we have been prepared well. We are mature, committed partners who are ready to conceive and care for the life of our child. Furthermore, we are deeply committed to teaching him or her about spirituality and sexuality. Whether natural or adoptive parents, we accept the sacred opportunity and responsibility of teaching our children about God's energy. We protect and guide the physical, emotional, mental, and spiritual growth of our children by enlightening them about healthy and spiritual sexual expressions.

ॐ

REFERENCES

Allen, G.P. The Sacred Hoop: A Contemporary Indian Perspective on American Indian Literature. In J. Rothenberg & D. Rothenberg (Eds.), *Symposium of The Whole*. Berkeley: University of California Press, 1983.

Berman, M. *The Reenchantment of the World*. New York: Holt Reinhart & Winston, 1981.

Deida, David. *Intimate Communion*. Deerfield Beach, Florida: Health Communication, Inc, 1995.

Deida, David. *Finding God Through Sex*. Boulder, Colorado: Sounds True, Inc., 2004.

Glendinning, C. *My Name is Chellis & I'm in Recovery from Western Civilization*. Boston: Shambhala, 1994.

Grof, S. *The Adventure of Self-Discovery: Dimensions of Consciousness and New Perspectives in Psychotherapy and Inner Exploration*. Albany, New York: State University of New York Press, 1988.

Hahnemann, S. *The Chronic Disease*. New Delhi: Jain, 1975.

James, W. *Varieties of Religious Experiences*. New York: Modern Library, 1902.

Kardiner, A. *The Traumatic Neurosis of War*. New York: Hoeber, 1941.

Kellogg, T. "The Roots of Addiction." [Cassette Recording]. Santa Fe, NM: Audio Awareness, 1991.

LaChapelle, D. *Sacred Land, Sacred Sex, Rapture of the Deep: Concerning Deep Ecology and Celebrating Life*. Durango, CO: Kaviki Press, 1988.

Laski, M. *Ecstasy: A study of Some Secular and Religious Experiences.* Bloomington, IN: Indiana University Press, 1962.

Muir Charles, & Muir, Caroline. *The Art of Conscious Loving.*
Mercury House, San Francisco, 1989.

Mumford, L. "The Case Against Modern Architecture."*Architect
ural Record 131*, April 1962.

Sewell, M. *Cries of the spirit: A celebration of Women's Spirituality.*
Rochester, VT: Park Street Press, 1991, 1.

Stace, W. *Mysticism and Philosophy.* New York: Harper & Row, 1960.

Swan, J. *Sacred Places: How the Living Earth Seeks Our Friendship.*
New York: Villard Books, 1990.

Wilson Sheaf, A. *Co-Dependence.* San Francisco: Harper & Row, 1986.

www.ingramcontent.com/pod-product-compliance
Lightning Source LLC
Chambersburg PA
CBHW032043080426
42733CB00006B/170